MOBSTER

The begining

Author   JAIME VINAS

All rights of reproduction from this work have been reserved. For which all reproduction from this book requires the written consent of his author.

YOUNG MOBSTER

INDEX

Int	7
1	9
2	23
3	36
4	58
5	98
6	139
7	164
8	209
9	216

YOUNG MOBSTER

Author: Jaime Vinas

Introduction.

The content of this work is based on a story created by the intellect of its writer exclusively, for which any similitude with any person or thing in real life is just casualty, a coincidence, the author excuse himself if such occurrence may arise, but is not his intention to copy a thing from real life, the all idea is to show the world that form of life described in the Bible for this world, is possible, to make it real, and it only show in what way it can to make is real that it only show a simple example, on how a small isle, can live with the help of the Almighty God, only, to live on the way, and the manner he desired that lived the nation daughter of Jacob, but they did not desired to follow, they never did, no matter how many times he invited them, they always refused and say: no.

The protector dome, that cover the isle are the arms of God from Heaven and earth, all the rest are that all have, the magic is the faith of the people, of nobody would come to make violence to a world protected by the God Father.

YOUNG MOBSTER

Chapter 1

Ms Maria awaked that day some kind overwhelmed that morning, had been raining a great deal on the morning at the end, in the little town of El Pedregal where she to live with her two sons, one always had her always exited. But he was the distinguish and the approved one, which had her, the one since he was a man, keep her up, living comfortable without nothing miss her.

But that night, have had a bad dream what had have worry, a dream about a presage from the past about her older son, what remind from memories from the pass, what remind her memories that she had about his bird; an astonished bird and fraithful that could overcome to Worm, because so, he had named them, because he uses to sleep twisted as a dead shrimp, but now this dream about something dark, she could not reach what to comprehend, and had her very worried.

Coming from the window were the first lights of the day, and no matter, was still raining, the light of the morning shadow was a little timid yet, while the water continue falling over the zinc a little old over the house, she pull up the shades, which cover her over her bed, and wrapped herself until the shoulders, to warm from that humidity **that the** sparkling of the rain produced over the zinc still, while she was thinking: "Lord, give me strength to support this that will overcome over mi son and over me.

Miss Maria was still considering over those minds that warring her and making her to fall almost in desperation, if at least would be me the natural son, but he is not, and I cannot distance me from that, I will not abandon him, will not leave him alone never, if I need to die with him, if will be so, I am ready to offer my life. The day had cleared already, it would be like seven in the morning from that winter morning day, here in the mountains of Guzman. And Miss

Maria had awaked she was a white woman, from about 50 years old, very sweet and loved in the little town of el Pedregal where they lived, she wore slightly, no matter still a little bit chili, the Quinta that serve them as home, build entirely of wood, a very old house. Build in the suburbs that Worn had acquired after he got his first arms smuggler, he has a big arms smuggler to supply, and s private office in the backuayard of his house, with privte office in the backyard of his house, the one he purchase from the first arms smuggler to the country in central America, and where Misrs Mary had lived with his two sons, no matter they were still young, Worn was 19 years old and Robert was 17, where young and brilliant and very awaked. Worn had become a smuggler in the business of fire arms smuggler, but somehow the police never could prove anything, and his brother, whom support him in everything him does, was still assisting high school and Worm had tilled him, he did not desired that him, got involved, at least until he become graduated from high school.

Worm is dynamically working on an order of arms, that had been ordered from the capitol of one of the countries of Central America, a country that find himself summed in a civil war with the government, so the police is frightfully behind of Worm for arrest him, because they suspect that he is the one that supply them with arms but, up to date they could not produce any evidence of such, especially, because that work is done while the ships are still over international waters, and they had not access on that distance, or have legal jurisdiction.

Miss Mary about of 9 o'clock is filling desperate, and alone as she was, is calling Robert who is still asleep, since he assist to school by the afternoons but want to talk to someone to be in company, she had her morning coffee already so, she is completely awake

Miss Maria - ! Roberto! ! Roberto!

Robert - What happened mama, why the loud, is still early, what, had something happened to Worn?

Miss Mary - No, my son, Worn is fine, he awaked about 5 o' clock, and went to see something to the farm of don Tomas his best man, but he is fine, you know that don Tomas is the chief there, of the army, and care for him and protect him, nothing happened to him, is that I feel worried, for something that do not reach to understand, and I need company, and as you are as mine doggy, I need you now here, come and drink your morning coffee that is already ready and hot still.

Roberto - Yes mama, allow me to brutish mine teeth, I feel with bad smell, will be almost be there, Good, already tell me what is that you feel? Tell me everything, you know that I am your confident, and also need to know facts in order to protect Worn if needed, I know he does not want to know that I'm getting involved in his matters, but suddenly he cannot get out. And need someone like me whom fit for any hole.

Miss Maria - Last night had a very ugly nightmare, like that I had the week of his first birthday when he got that high fever that the doctors who attend him could not find any explanation, it's got until 42 degrees and last for 2 days, and at the 3 err day awaked already cured **without** fever at all, only the temperature was still by the 87 degrees, without any health problem, and had stay like the same, he say he is always hot and that is why he had to install that air conditioner so powerful to his truck, and always put it so cool in the SUV that he has, so I do not like to go with him for that, he is always hot. That head do not abandon him at any minute.

Robert - Now I understand mama, but do you have any info of why of those dreams? Is there anything that you may thing now that will happen? What was the reason he was for to don Tomas? Did he tell you anything else?

Miss Mary - Well, he told me something, like the work that he had to deliver, but no detail at all, nothing specific, you know that Tomas is not going to help him for he to stole the army, because it would be like to put him to stole to himself. He is the maximum authority, but could be because the army is going to receive any order of guns recently, and he want to know it, to still it before it come to the army deposit, I guess, because had no reasons to believe so either. The truth is that I am out of focus and worried for that premonition.

Roberto - Mama, Do you know that Worm is building a construction in the farm that he purchased last week? And that arrived some seeds from Colombia yesterday? I believe he will plant them right away. Because he told me that under any circumstance, do not show up over there, because he is making a plantation of casaba in the greenhouse near of the casaba planted at free air over there, and is going to look very nice and pretty with this frame like aluminum and metal with that colored metal screen. Is going to be very elegant with the green leaves of the casaba is going to be a very nice plantation. What I see is that the greenhouse is higher than all others in the country, it has the higher of 4 story building, about 10 yards told.

Miss Mary - He was commenting that he is going to make a remedy for all those who intoxicate with food and beverages and beside is going to use to get cure his problem of permanent fever that he has.

Robert - Where did Worn learn those medicine knowledge he has mama? Do you know that?

Miss Mary - Well Robert, Worn was a very smart boy, look at what age he got to start to smuggler, and he has make it very well, never has confrontations with the police, or the army, much less, they accuse him, but they could present any proof, nothing at all to him, from the money he has, about 5 million dollars, cannot probe nothing either neither the precedence, the government even have any infraction, or has stole any arms to the government, his robbery, had been always over international waters, or to the government suppliers before they had delivered them.

Roberto - Mama, when said Worn he would return? Did he say something about that?

Miss Maria - No Roberto, he said do not worry, he would come to have breakfast with us, but as he do not feel hunger, maybe breakfast will be lunch for him. Listen to that noise, look like it damages something to the truck. There is Worn, Lets prepare the breakfast.

Worn - Mama!. Roberto! Do not worry for breakfast, I brought it prepared from the cafeteria, I brought casaba, fried eggs, fried cheese, milk with chocolate, as you like, some bananas with some delicious meat. Did not resist the temptation and gave ate little bit as a test! Well, I have too much work for today, I was talking with my best man for he to assigned me a group of soldiers, in order to watch the buildings of the farm, because the police as always is watching me and bothering me, do not go to damage the plantation that are in the greenhouses that no matter they are for legal medicines, with that we are going to have a much better business, maybe not need to sell smugglers arms no more, that promise to be a very great success, my dearest brother, the little plants already brought, that spread system that maxim, had installed last week is making a tremendous good work, but come on, have your breakfast, hear is everything ready.

Miss Maria - What have happened to your truck, that we here a tremendous noise from the motor my son?

Worm - That was only the Muffler that leaving my Good father's farm, open land, after that long last rain, a tire fall into a hole, a rock probable hit the muffler, and something fall apart, and now after breakfast will go to the shop to fix it. I am not going to hold the breakfast any longer, because this is delicious, too good.

They sat together at the table with that delicious breakfast that Worn had bring full with all his love and caress, with also all his affections for his mother and his brother, after a short time, there was nothing over the table, they ate the all thing, and if there was something else, they have it to disappear too, no matter they were completely satisfy.

Miss Maria - We want to know, what plans do you have with that farm you had purchase? Do you have any explanation to give for the government?, do you have already any explanation to justify in case they make an investigation, because we do never had that kind of money.

Worn - Mother, live that to me, with my good father we know exactly how to answer those questions he back me up on whatever I may need, you are aware of that, no?

After that long and heavy rain, from last night and that morning, the sun had show up, radiant, the sky was completely blue, with some white clouds, nothing of gray clouds, all clear, it was now all clear, and it was unparallel beauty, as they are only a few days so beautiful.

Time start running out, after three months had pass after the agricultural constructions, and the equipment used to set up, the plants of casaba and cocaine have been grow up a little those of casaba, were growing a little, and those of cocaine, were very big already, and starting to grow the flowers, soon they were going to produce the little fruit that produce the seeds, for ground theme out, to produce the typical almost white, like a little yellow crème, that show up they are like sick, but really its the natural color, like wet talc powder and dried again on a newly account.

A few days after, in his house, with a pitch, with some liquid inside from clear color and offer to his matter to drink while say:

Worm - Try this, and you also Robert, you that had a few days ago some digestions problems, maybe from something that were warring you and you Robert, so you do not get to worry for anything.

Both were served a glass from those drink that were energetic and delicious, effervescent also, with a divine flavor, right away, it was not only a delicious flavor, that offer vitality right away felt both very healthy, the mother said that she was not worried and Robert said there was no reason for him to get worry, that drink had have hard to convince so he get not worry, that he probably defeated to anyone who come to bring complications.

Right away, went to the hardware store, to get a bunch of screws for wood, some woods, flat top, and long, saw, screws and hammer, on her side Miss Maria brought and pick up some little bottles that pick up from the back of the house, like 10 of them, and prepared serape of different flavors and have been filled from the liquid that Worn had prepared, it was an energetic drink, and at the same time it was medicinal, it was a remedy with flavor of fruits, that now offer to the general public at a low price, lower from those they sell the beverages at the bar, and the grocery stores, but there was nowhere in the town, with a better flavor, not get even with them.

Roberto called one of his friends that has some drinks last night, and ask to try that drink Worn had in the bottles, they got a glass and the friend drank, call into another from last night party, and another, and they all got cured and thanks, subsequently, for that drink, like magic that have been show up suddenly they notify to the people in the town, whom were forming lines in front of that cart, which have just been build and they decided to paint it among all, together right there. Everyone went to the hardware store, and bring paints from different color, and give to the cart a very colorful, like little children likes, red, white, clear blue, dark blue, dark green, and clear, brown clear, chocolate, endless, a wide variety of colors and all and them felt happy, playing, and labor giver, ready to collaborate with everything necessary, to the girls it came to happen, to prepare food for all, on a number who already pass of the 40 people, but they felt so happy, and motivated, that they felt so happy and motivated that they need to celebrate for that divine medicine and delicious from Worm, that he had bring from the leaves and heirs from the constructions he had build that until now was something like magic and nobody could and was able to prepared it, only Warm, but as he was so lovely and friend of all of them, they allow him the formula as his secret.

Chapter 2

The good moment started that night, when Worm went to the Groans(Vicente) bar and start to drink beer, he drank 20, after what he realized that he had left the money at home so, had nothing to be able to pay for the bill before to be able to exit the doors of the bar, and the Groans told him that he had to pay, before to be able to exit, because he was been offering beers to any one, that 20 was that he had drank, but he had spread among all, no matter he new have to pay before the be able to live the place, and he knew he had offered all, like 220 bottles, and no matter he knew Worm used to pay fine, he doesn't know if he had enough to be able to liquidate such elevated bill.

Groans' wife, a fat lady, more than the double than her husband, called the police, who arrived immediately, and decided to Worm, but Worm had bring his special drink and was giving to the polices whom where his fri**ends, one of them** tried and recommend it to the others, so, all of them following him, and drank and continue drinking, they make in quantities, as for do not to want to arrest Worm, and told Groans to let him go, and in the morning he will come back and pay the bill, that if he do not pay, they would pay for him.

The bar was such disordered, until the noise get to the police delegation, and the lieutenant showed up, send by supervisor Perez from the police who looking to return the peace to the town, who get disordered with any little disorder, did not desired, that the people to make a giber damaged, beyond a few people drunk, or any other, taking care of the opportunity of the disorder, Roberto scaled from the bar, went to his house, opened the worm's safe, where his mother used to guard his money, took a bunch of money and came quickly back to Worm, where a tumult of more than 300 people had get together, among consumers, polices and curious, once there, he got Worm, gibe him the money and said loud:

Robert - One beer to anyone who likes one, and gives me the bill Groan, to pay it right now, that the money had come already in order to pay it.

The total of the bill was 17.523.50 that hi paid immediately, and still has enough to pay another round of some 100 bottles more. So the inventory from the bar came almost totally empty, the people do not used to drink so much there, the last beers had to drink them warm because there was not time enough for they to chill up enough due to the high demand in so little time, which it had never be, until that date and never was, at no less for something that happen a short time after, but no more from Worms hands.

At time, Worm and Robert came out their faces to the street, there, showed up the Police supervisor with the intention of to find out the result from that revolt, and at sight of Worm was out, felt the desired of arrest him, but his cellular phone rang and it was the national chief of the army who remind him of taking very good care or him, because he is his **godchild who is untouchable for him**, that leave him alone, and free, in peace.

It was in that way when our protagonist, result freed from the revolt due to the careless from the groans who thought that Worm would turn dishonest and slow to pay suddenly after 19 years from been honest and have been living with dignity among them, but with a heat as he always were showing after 1 year of age, he turned and got two cold beers, to go drinking they by the way, he asked for them to put scratched iced inside and to put it inside of the bottled so they cold off from that infernal heat which do not detach him at any time.

Right away they got inside the truck Land Cruiser, at high 4x4 of worm they turn the air conditioner, at a high speed and coldest, until got some fresh from that terrible heat for the two brothers, mainly the older brother which was the most affected always, they returned home where was Miss Mary, sat at the entrance, sat a little, and stand up, then sat again, waiting for every second the arrival of her two sons, when saw the truck coming by the front street of her house, felt a great peace, she felt a great peace and got a big relaxation and sat with peace in her rocking chair.

The boys came close to the house and she told them:

Miss Mary - Listen, you have me desperate, what was that you arm where the Groans, you know that man is not the one you can trust, do not offer him any excuses or opportunity of arm a scandal.

Worm - Yes mama, already we understood lucky me, because Roberto is more squeeze and got to escape to pick up the money to pay for the bill, and so the thing was solved otherwise we would have to get all police drunks and the bill would be even higher because those guys are many and drink a lot, like crazies.

Miss Mary - Well, put the truck in the garage, that truck cost a lot of money and all the thieves should be checking on you, awaiting for a chance to intent to steeled it, and you now it very well.

Right away Roberto takes the keys from the hands of Worm, and put it in the garage of the house, the truck of double traction and special air conditioning, and enclose it with key, and give then to Worm, so, he delivered then.

Worm - You know how to drive very well; soon will help you so, so you can get your driving license, so you can be able to drive your own truck.

Roberto - Yes, but that the air conditioning be regular, no so cold as yours, please, yes little brother?

Worm - When your turn comes, it will be as you please mi brother, as you like it, all the details, it will be as you like; it would be yourselves who chooses it at don Marino store.

Miss Mary - Oh, yes Worm, that it would be like yours, but not blinded, and that do not cold that much, because Robert is who takes me everywhere I want to go, because you are always into your things, is to suppose that now, with that farm and those elixirs you are preparing now secretly we are going to count less even now, at on purpose of those medicinal, the doctor Gonzales want you take to him some samples of those elixirs, because he want to inspect them to make some analyzes them and he want to talk with you because nobody is going to make the regular consults and the people do not complain on anything. If you are going to make him to bankrupt with that disloyal competence that you have him installed, and making smuggling drinks.

Worm receipt a phone call in his cell phone, and go to answer it to the end of the back yard, under a mango tree, the big one where he has a basement and an office hidden where you can enter under a secret door inside of the trunk of the mango tree, where you can not listen to anything of from that who want to enter, or exit anything from what want to exit to make a little noise from that door, is like a hidden secret, to find out how to encounter how to open the door. There are to find how to open it, there are to know exactly to find how to open the knob of the door, and you know exactly where it is, because nothing can be see it of the very well hidden it is. Also it has another entrance, coming from a closet inside of the house from to sleep room of Worm, coming by a tunnel to get into that basement.

Worm - The next week you will be purchasing Roberto's truck because it entered a big order of arms to the country of the neighbor who got into civil war and they told that when they'll got some money they ask borrow from the empire in turn, they will buy many more arms to depose then from power, and when they get into it, they are not going to need any more, they will use him as a counselor and they will pay him very well, this will be in pay for this you are doing for them now in the difficult time for them, who do not know whom to trust to.

Miss Maria - Worm, do you have something here hidden?

Worm - No, not here, but you know, in the deposit where Gustavo lived there is where I saved them, together with the corn, also there are containers with coffee, there are also containing ammunitions there, as all that is very heavy, and all weight a lot, get combined and is being sold combined to the people, and that merchandise is always entering and exiting and maintain a level all the time very well balanced at all the time, my merchandise is always ready to be delivered at any time is needed.

They asked for an order of coffee and corn and goes directly to over there, we sell guns and ammunitions as been agricultural products and they pay us the additional money under the table, separate and detached.

Miss Mary - Worm, mi son so smart, he has made himself a business man that is so young, nobody suspects that your business are ileitis, but as they present themselves on the routes, as honest.

Worm - Yes mama, I sell arms during the day, and deliver them in front of the police, that is where my warehouse is placed, nobody can suspects that inside those sacs of coffee or corn are hidden all an armament ready to make the war to any country.

That country trust me, because I have never defrauded them, from the first time we go to them to delivered that they need and the way they received them got supersized and I told them that the meeting point for future delivered would be in front of the police on my city, so we do not need to hide, how it looks a legal business, honest, and there is nothing to hide, or to feel afraid of.

Worm - Those sacs are on very good quality, and are wrapped with another sac in case anyone get broken, the one outside do not allow the arms to come out since they are in double enfold.

Miss Mary - Worm, tell me about how many sacs do you keep in the warehouse inventory?

Worm - Oh mama, like 2000 of coffee and like 10000 of corn, because we sell a lot more from the one of corn, but the guns only there are 200 and 500 in corn, I have a mark to make a difference from the others, that only i can distinguish because there is a reactive tint that let see differentiate in colors with some special lens, used only to separate the sacs. Tomorrow is coming a ship full of arms for the army of this country, and I have them sold, so I need to get them tonight, also, arrive tonight another ship that I purchased from Brazil loaded with coffee, that one will pass as Colombian, that I sell much at a higher price than the Brazilian, over there I pretend get the arms that I will take from deep sea through a team of divers who will surprise the ship that will come from France with my armament.

Worm take out his special cell phone he has in the rear pocket and the one he used to call his technical team and tell them:

Worm - It would be that date, about 10 o'clock, the ship will enter the Caribbean sea which is the place that take the heavy boxes, and by at night will take the heavy sacs containing their merchandises, and the next day we will discharge the corn and the coffee, he will be there for help to pack them well, and hope that when I arrived there they would be in top of the ship, and ready to do their work, because he has his time measured.

Employed - Fine, all under the control, when get to the warehouse, have all ready, the ship will get to the warehouse this afternoon, and will be discharged during the night. After tonight, we will take some vacations, because coffee, enter in recession, because finish the pickup time and will not going to be more for a period of 6 months, after this, that is the reason of the additional shipment.

Said Virgilio, the inventory supervisor, that a new customer had call to buy corn, and coffee, all they need, he does not want to buy from your competitor, because he knows the quality you are offering is superior and also want to buy his elixir of happiness that you are manufacturing

Worn has the phrase about the elixir, he says it is aphrodisiac, and is good to keep in effect the love relations among the young persons and also among the not that young persons, to the old persons they put those old people, as children's very strong as when they were younger, they are exporting from starting about 1000 cases in small size, but the united states have stopped them in the harbor until the department of agriculture, extend the permit to enter to private warehouses.

All other countries of the Caribbean has no problem to let it in, as it be rice and beans, as they have seem demonstrations of functionality, of self and the tasty it is, how delicious is the flavor, and how it do not produce any counter reaction to the people who drink it, and do not have any impediment, that is why they are producing an impressive quantity of profit in sales, so much, that the United States had sent only one ship and have not go across from customs yet, but unto other countries, we are sending daily ships is a great success, but the American people are checking it in, before to let enter, and the drinking had been retained and the drinks were been taking to the laboratories only one case for those analysis and investigation.

Worn say take it easy, they know what is in there, and that most to be pacific and slow, do not make too much movement, the calm is the way that give the God advise that thing has to be taking care of, and is the way for the think that go for having success, and is the way that her mother had educated to solve all his facts, that never lose it, or say so to his representatives

Chapter 3

That afternoon, after had discharge the guns, come a white Sir, toll, about some 6 feet high in a white stretch limo and himself alone sat in the rear seat, doing a great expectative, and pretending to be a big deal, and asking to have a meeting with the owner of the elixir, because his company desire to buy it all at any price he chooses, he want to be the universal distributor exclusive, worldwide and he can set any price at all, because he will accept it and buy it all, anyway. Presumptions, this that dislike to Worm at all so, he is showing no inters in talking to him at all in absolute.

Finally, Worm got into the warehouse, and the Canadians saw him and salute very friendly, saying to him:

Blondie - Sir, it is a great pleasure to make your acquaintance, I am here to give you peace on the distribution of your elixir, I am ready to take care of the worldwide distribution on it, before than the pharmaceutical taking care of, and offer you for the marketing offer you only a very little part of what you really deserve for the merchandise of this excellent product, which you are producing just like that.

Worm said to the secretary of the office to offer all of them a good cup of coffee, and him too, so he can feel like home, maybe decide to go quickly as him had considered.

Bud he is decided, and immediately, asks him for:

Blondie – what place can we use to talk softly, because I have wonderful plans and are to your disposition, he is open to accept any kind of proposal he wants, and is open widely the proposal he decide, because the references he have about the product are good and the success is warranted, so they only are waiting for he's only proposal only. Worm tell him that in all the town there is no place like that he is talking about, that's what all of them do, because, in that town are poor and simple persons and they do not use to go to any particular place to surprise the others, to pretend in front to another, and that is why we are inviting him to drink a cup of coffee at his office, because is what we used with friends here.

The Canadian speak about the bar in front of the park, in the capital, where the other day form a kind of revolt and he knows it was against you the situation, it is well know. But do not worry, he has how to pay for the bill to pay whatever be the total, he has money to pay for all. And he has money to pay him in advance for a good deal of merchandise to start the distribution that he is ready to charter the plain for return and take it loaded with the elixir, to prepare all that may fit in the plain with him, they desire to start as soon as possible, in Canada are already working in the distribution channels worldwide, that is about to be sold and offered in groceries stores, bars, supermarkets, endless list, all kind of possibilities of commerce, as medicine and soft drinks.

Worm wishes to accept the invitation, so they go to the bar of the groans and start to drink cocktailsWorm start to talk th, at is a common and normal thing, like a combination of drugs and natural drinks with medicine, that is for to cure the people because his people are poor people and they cannot pay for high costs of the medicine to cure for all the sickness, so, he has a plan to save the people of the all world, but is not with money, but with love, that this plan can take effect, if they make it that way, they will cure them, it will make them more contaminated, and make them even more sick people, making them more difficult to cure, because that medicine do not work as the pharmaceutical medicines, but from the love of God, from the God in heaven, who is not a commerce man of an unscrupulous one, but one of love and happiness giver that is on this way as him will commerce with that and had been considered as good, and have considered that no matter if he will filled his pocket with money, that he is going to be able of help, because on what he is manufacturing is destiny not to make himself rich, but to make him kind and good for the others.

The Canadian Blondie is not looking to understand anything from the way of talking of Worm, he is inserted on commerce more than simple merchandise and have ordered the impression of simple pamphlets for its distribution, and in his country are waiting for that, to take directly to hospitals, health centers for all the nation and he is waiting for all nation that all sick people would be cured the very first day that medicine arrive to the country, and that he is expecting going together in him in the same plain, that he will take it back in the same plain that will take back the happiness, to his country, this is going to be a big party to celebrate.

Worm go with the Canadian to the bar of the Groan(Vicente) to take some drinks in particular Cognac, and the most expenses drinks they can find any way the blonde assure be going with money enough he has then for sacs that he is able to pay any amount that be required and will not accept that Worm pay anything because is for him the right to make the invitation and also pay for the bill when presented, because he has orders to proceed that way and more if necessary, then Worn get into the white limo and part softly to the bar of Vincent.

Once there, star to the drinks, they order by bottles entire and are so many the bottles that they expend them cases, everyone who enter to the bar are invited to drink with and by the blonde who one to be simpatico to the people also want they think that he can with anything. That he is a very powerful man that has well appropriate of the money of the world, any way he pays with American dollars and the money exchange is at the rate of exchange of 100 pesos for 1 dollar, and before that he is not afraid to any number. Them expend is raisin, and also they start to order food, like lobsters, shrinks and anything they want, Worm or the visitors and curious. Vincent remind Worm what happened the other day and that:

Vincent - I do not want that happen again, because I do not credit in the bar food or drinks, nobody lives my place without liquidate the bill before. So we do not have problems I remind, have it present, the policies of the bar is not change and either is going to change with blonde or without him, because the blonde it was you who brought here I had not seem him before, and maybe do not see him again after this, and he respond me for him, because I never had seem him.

Worm - I do not know him, and you know I always pay my debts, no worry, relax stay quiet, mean while, the cups are filling every time more, the people of the town have been calling the others and the bar is completely full, there is not an empty chair including the backs of the bar also are full and also are bringing chairs from the neighbors and sitting in the sidewalks and over the streets there is a total full, the bar is putting already hot, not only because of the body human heat, but for the alcohol, and smoke more and more to charge of the Blonde the cigarettes of the bar got finish completely and Vincent send his son to the center of town for more, but they are finished also and also sent to the center of the capitol for more, but there is no more they are finished with all of them there is no more for the sell in the town or the capital.

With the exited animas, the blonde start to pull out the contract, he has redacted from Ottawa, for worm to signed it, He will not change anything or waited for him to read it, this is Gestapo way you signed and that is it.

Blonde – Here I put the conditions, you are not able to negotiate, because I am who pay, and I put the condition, that is it.

He give the contract to Worm and this put himself to observe it, turn the first page and the blonde hold it and close and put in the first order it was, after that, open the contract in the last page, give a pen to him and say:

Blonde – That is the only page you need to see, because is the one where you are going to put your signature, what you are is a farmer and I am here who put the conditions, because a farmer will say to me what I have to do.

Worm is altering himself, because this guy is insulting him little by little but is little by little how the hen eat and full themselves and also get fat, and worm had get fat already, and he find that much enough.

Worm – Look Mr. Blonde, I have listened too much from you and yours piggy advises, here we do not eat pigs, because our God had forbidden them, and we are respectful and we do show respect for him, but you have become crazy, and you are became like a pig for us, so, that will not going to be possible to eat you, I need to go to the bathroom to evacuate, and this is the paper I will use when finished, when I get out from there, do not want to see you again, so, check your sacs, pay the long bill you have made and comeback the way you came, because probably that is the only place where you are welcome, because here you are not, and will not be tomorrow either.

He left, hold the contract and get himself into the bathroom and stay over there for a long time, at finish of what come out smiling, and with a soft face and a sweet smiled, as he had not drink anything before, but the blonde stood there, Worm do not have the contract, because he done what he did what he have promised he would do, when blonde saw him with empty hands, the blonde got a colorized, for all the alcohol he had drink, lift the hands as for hold Worm for the neck and push him against the wall that was a the left or to the right, because they had taken a corner table and he sat together by the corner, he took evasive form and the blonde loss the balance, and passed over him, fallen to the floor as big and toll he was, without to produce any damage to the property.

When Vincent saw the riot forming, called the police so they come to suffocate this disorder and restore the order in the bar, there was a patrol who was doing their round by the zone, and made presence in place, once there, ask for what is going on?

Vicente wife – That blonde was making disorder, menace every one with hit Worm because he does not sign the contract and tried to fight with him, because he had broken the contract, and I want you to take him out of the bar, after pay the bill that was near of the 150,000 pesos, because they had drink everything that was in the bar and ate the all food.

The police addressed then to the blonde asking him:

Police – Are you going to pay the bill or what?

Blonde – Well, look to me that this is going to be or what, because this guy do not want to do business with me, if no, here it will be a tragedy because to me nobody do that, I am the law wherever I go and where I am, is done what I say.

Sergeant Berta — The law there are put by then, and is already done, and everyone is free to do what is convenient, it looks like what you want and say, is not convenient to Worm because you are too radical in your ways, and over there are not very welcome those with your character or manners and surely that is why that Worm do not have please you in all you have propose to him.

The blonde stand up, and address himself to the exit and say:

Blonde — Tomorrow It will be in this little island the marine of Canada, and the army of the Unites States, then you will see what happened, this will not finished like that, I am a very powerful man, and are ready to use my power and influence, because Worm is putting on risk, the all pharmaceutical industry of the world for a too little substance insignificant and that is something the world cannot tolerate, that little thing has to disappear, I came to negotiate a friendly agreement, and pay well for what think that can cost, but that cannot be continue using that cheap thing to cure the all the world for that are the pharmaceutical products that are manufactured around the world for real rich industrials, no by farmers like worm.

The blonde live and get into his white big limo and live quickly to the airport, where a jet on is awaiting with the air conditioning on, put the car in the back and part from there, get into the pox compartment and quickly depart on the way to the Canada.

While in the bar of Vicente is forming another riot, like the other that form with Worm like 2 weeks ago, but now the bill is real big, then that amount do not make Worm to be timid for nothing, is not too much for Worm, and newly Robert arrive and ask his brother the nature of the situation, and he say, that go and pick 160 thousand pesos from his safe in his bedroom, in order to liquidate the bill of the bar that the blonde have generate, but Vicente say that he cannot live the place until the bill have been liquidated, that he knows that are his conditions, and call his armed men and strong for them take charge and enforce his orders, that Worm knows that is so how it work in his bar.

The police then speak, interfering the process, and say:

Police – Robert was not here when that was expend and that Worn will stayed here, been the responsible for the bill, as Vicente had been claimed all the time, but you let the blonde escape without paying, been the main responsible for the payment, ten Vicente say:

Vicente – Nobody will live this place, I have armed men for that, for nobody lives without paying first, nobody will live from my business that is now in a dangerous situation. now is almost bankrupt and that bill is paid off or is paid off. He knows he has to pay, and at to enter to the bar must to have with him the money to fix the bill. Those are Vicente Rules, and in my bar is obbey.

Again the police make his intervention:

Police – This is an special situation, Worm do not invite the Blonde, was to the inverse, it was the blonde who made the bill and Worm had not denied to pay, only the money is not here to be able to do it, to make an exception.

Vicente – I say no, my rule is that, and it has been the same and need to obey it, and nobody will make me to change my way. Because that had been like that since the first day that I opened the doors of these place, this I made this building with my own hands, I erect those walls myself, and are strong, because no group will turn it down because their are strength and they will hold down to all those people until that the bill of 150,000 be paid and a tip of at least one cent be added to it. Rules Vicente.

Worm stands up and makes a gets and say:

Worn – I am full from to hear this ugly to lunch cries.

Then, arm like some kind of collective hypnotism and all see Worm like he is a giant of 15 feet's tall and his skin have change like skin of gorilla and his eyes are ground up and the mouth is very big, and do not talk but launch strong cries, and all are afraid because are strong voices likes are hear in the movie King Kong in his inauguration, by the year 1936 when had his love one in the high of the Empire State Building when the tower was recently build. This live walking from the bar at giving passes causing a kind of earthquake in the country, that was felt coast to coast, from north to south, and from east to west the all country felt that quake, that is why they realize that something really important have been happening, because in that island had never felt an earthquake, this was the first that happened, because there were not any geological fails, in the island, or on the surroundings.

A National alarm is given for to prosecute of Worn, not only for the bill of Vicente, but for he has converted himself in a monster that have afraid the people, and has revolt the national peace, and there is to catch him at anyway because he jas disrupt the national peace, so, they are using like 100 thousand member of the armed forces, and put some others 400 thousand from the national reserve, because there is to catch him whatever it takes, dead or alive, shut to kill at sight is considered extremely dangerous, do not take any chance, keep a safe distance from him.

Worm knows how the situation how is, the best place where he can be should be the mountains, where his aunt, the sister of his mother that is for him like his second home where he lived for more than one year when his mother got seriously six and she feed him very well, plus he felt very loved due to her tender love, and soft character and sweet, her fine modals that he could never forget, nonetheless, he never return to visit her in all those years but he was sure once arrive there, he will be fine receipt, he was sure of it.

Worm pass and stop at the shop of William, who had be always his friend, no matter that he has never need him as a professional, no matter, they have been very close one from the other, from heart to heart.

William – What was that to happen and what do you want from me?

Worm – I am in a lot of troubles, take me out of town, I want to go to 60 kilometers, north to the house of my aunt, my mother's sister, where I will be safe. The police or the army will not see or recognize to both in the truck because I have some hypnotic powers to avoid that happen, do not worry for that.

William closes the shop, and put a sign closed until tomorrow, and live with Worm to the exit of the town, north exit, turn in one of the main roads to the right and are addressed to the north exit from El Pedregal, this, no matter is not a big town, either is very small, there live likes 50 k people, the country has like 10 millions of residents, and compare to the capitol with 150 k people, is light populated, and the people is very disseminated alongside the territory. People used to work different types of work, in the field there are agriculture, and in the cities, are industries of different kinds, in that order the people live very fine, and is disseminated everywhere very happyly, they have all work and the unemployment do not reach the 1 per cent of the population they live reasonably happy and do not require of medicine doctor or veterinary even because the medicine of Worm cure all the sickness that get present in persons or animals, and is for that he is so much appreciated until for those who have never male his acquaintance yet.

The reason for that the blonde got so hot is because Worm was menacing with make a worldwide distribution, that will cause the pharmaceutical industry worldwide to collapse, because due to all the quemicals and acids use in the manufacture for their costly medicinal products, will collapse, due that the world no longer will take their costly and dangerous poisons, with those that have been making of killing little by little and causing terrible sickness, like Aids, Influence, Cancer, and other sickness more that will be needed a long list that will not fit on this page. Writing it in friendly phrases.

It have been form blocks in the main roads and all the ways of exit of the city of El Pedregal, have been put super vigilance in all supermarkets to avoid that the mother of worm and his brother could buy food so he can escape from that search that the army and the police have armed.

Meanwhile, William have advance a lot, and is found outside of town, have pass by two positions revisions and they have salute Worm as by the name of David, William's son, ant this, surprised, ask Worm that:

William – David Is not here, and they are confusing him with you, how weir situation is this.

The captain of the army have call don Rupert, the English so, he help them by bringing his Doberman dogs that he has and always have put to the service of the army, but that have never presented a need to be used them, that now finally have a chance of use them for the first time and the English go happy for that. When the second world war, his dogs help very much when the prisoners escaped from the camps and they always find them quickly, so he was very proud of them. (of course it was not those animals, but their grandparents).

By that moment, Worm is find far from the reach of his prosecutors whom are still reaching in the city of El Pedregal, now, came to the station Jacinto, a young man called Jacinto, who always have a controversies with Worm and was desired him was catch, only because has envy for him, and say to the captain that he has an aunt in the mountain, and surely he has go to get refuge. over there because is not too fare, and is at a good distance from there, and there are many different places over there where he can be easily hidden, the farm is very big and only her and his employees live in around 50 kilometers round, that may be not easy to find him over there because there are all kinds of traps and caves, that is a special place for that a revolutionary can do from his, and keep refugee.

Miss Mary who have notice the running by everywhere, and finally have get the complications formed at Vicente's bar and his son is been prosecuted, and they have arrested Robert to make oppression for he surrender but that he had been freed because the police cannot make oppression with that objective, because that is violation to his civil rights and for disposition of the president of the island had been freed and is on the way to his house with his mother in this moment. The chief of the army have not come out on his help because he is in a farm and had not been able to be reached.

Now, at seem the prosecution live in the city, for the rural area, the army realize that the best they can do is to get a plan to make that Worm surrender and get him to comeback to be the peace man he used to be his all life and right away start to transmit news by the radio and television, that the army is searching for a conversation with Worm, to get him to peacefully return to her mother's home Because him had been always that have not been afraid that as soon as he stepped in the grass of his mother back yard, the all prosecution is finished, and will work to be keep like that.

Before all this team of publicity, is conclude with Worm return to his mother's house accompany always for his friend William the Mechanic that not live him alone at any time, so, all this have been finished with the situation, prosecution what start with two intransigencies, first, the blonde Canadian and then the one of Vicente from the bar of the town, we saw how those intransigencies dedicated to the people make the wishes of someone by the power and wishes and that violence do not work.

Once again the country return to his peaceful routine, Worm comeback to his warehouse of Coffee, corn and the serape, to continue with its distribution, lets remind he has a remission of guns what to do, what is at to the date the central business no matter this has been relatively diminished, and the sell of fire arms had been diminished in comparison of the Sirope, which had been raising that is sell daily everywhere, and is becoming every time more popular, remember that is not only medicine, but is a delicious refreshment, so it sale in great amounts everywhere, until to eat with the foods is been drinking by the people it is been packed already in an enormous packet plant that has been build in the zone of the farm where the elixir is produced and the cocaine is planted. The serape is manufactured with liquid sugar from corn, concentrate of fruits juice, imported from Brazil, so, is a refreshment drink completely natural.

Chapter 4

And is like that how Worm convert himself from a criminal trafiquer with firing arms in a industrial producer of medicinal fruit juice, he come back to be again the new national idol that all of the inhabitants of Gusmani wish and feel proud of be compatriots of him. From whom feel a great and profound and difficult to explain proud, but the daily operations work from the best way, and with some form that all the countries of the world would like to poses, but what happened is that there is only one Worm in the all world, and cannot by interchanged, what happened is that to contraries this, his juice is going to be put at the disposition in all countries of the world helping as vaccines to prevent practically the all world so, in order to fixed all the sixpences and wounds that are produces and happened everywhere, and the last discovered is for that the sirope or worm be serving of preventive for wounds and lesions such as sickness.

All this looks fantastique, but the real experience says that there is no better, the dolence and sickness practically have been disappear everywhere first, for the zones of countries more poor and are advancing to the rich countries because there are not monetary discrimination for the cure or prevention of problems, because all the citizens o the world are sons of God and he is decided to care of all of them, good and bad, and any color of skin.

Worm is converting himself in the richest man in the all world, his income for the sale of the coffee, corn grain, and the medicinal serape, and nutritive with flavor to all kind of fruit, the concentrate juice, imported from Brazil, although are very numeral, give an extra gallon for every 10 gallons, after adding to the serape special from the greenhouse, all in the island feel highly proud of having Worm as a co citizen and are offering prizes and recognition practically daily, but Worm, no matter he doesn't want that, either put objections for them to continue offering others, the case is all his walls and tables are full and do not fit another more.

Several times he has addresses to the media of communications in table of conferences, communicating that he doesn't want any other and they should not offer any additional, because whatever he does is limited to the wishes of the Lord God of heaven and earth, they should not to continue offering those recognition, but whatever he does is limited to the wishes of God on earth, for the Good of man and women and children.

Worm – Is the duty of a father with his sons what he does, please do understand, this does not continue taking the lead in opposition to the Creator as always the world did from before I would coming to it. The world have been always rebel and the people do not understand the common sense and continue always doing what their want they should do, no matter that the other party be in disappointing, and this is the detailed on which Worm be a little in disappointment with his co citizens, because at point of pass unseeing, nevertheless the others want him to be the most popular and known among all, and over all.

In the all island the ambulance service got discontinue, which are been used in the future for public transportation of passenger in the city, in place of transporting sick persons, this is done because there is no more sick people or hurt at all, they had extract the beds, and converted in very comfortable seats, putting back up parts for the back part of the body, so the people put sit belts and stay safe and comfortable at travel and brake violently.

With all this in mind, the accident in the island are eventually and never bring as consequences, death people, only hurt lights that are normally cured with the worm's serape which cure that instantly, and is get anywhere, there is no suffering in the country besides all the population take it wherever they go because they know his cure power and because is vital for the daily living.

How good the peace had return to El Pedregal! Says Juan Tomas the medicine doctor of the town that now is a simple commerce man whom dedicate to sell Worm's serape. Since that day, the doctor decided that would keep provisions, like in a intimate depository in case of Worm may have something that cause any other trouble and may need of them like it happen during the prosecution of the other day, and let it know to Worm in the first chance he got.

Worm was not a man of many words, but was a man of much action, so what he did was take several cases of serape of different flavors and gave it to the doctor and say, this is my answer to your words you say to me, and is how I appreciate my friends the thinks they do for my good will.

In the same way as the doctor of the town did to protect him in that occasion, and to would rotate the inventory from time to time, some other persons did likewise the doctor did, and let the doctor know, in case his notation do not be enough some time, this will give to the good Worm a feeding safety more adequate.

The town love Worm, no matter do not know him, no matter they do not know him, if they would know him it would be probable another thing, maybe they wouldn't know anything, it is possible that they no even would like address the sight, because that is the way the people reaction and always had been like that, despise the of whatever come from God. At time of coming of the night, Worm return home with the mother and brother, getting peace from a difficult day what happened the blonde Canadian, who swear that this case will not finished like that they would take the case to continue, and it would be worse now than that day.

The final comment of the Canadian blonde come to the ears of the president, who was the only person with quality for peaceful that blonde dictator and arrogant that needed a lesson of behavior and of good been besides, he had been as no sense and disrespectful who do not tried or desire show a doses minimum to should be the north and his first option for overall. The president send a diplomatic to the United Nations in New York and call on the phone to the Prime Minister of Canada and to the president of the Senate of the United States, and to the president of the United States to complaint for the behavior of his representative.

At time of talk with the president of the island express to him the doubt that was remain over his enterprises what produce the medicines and over the future situation of the medical class in the world due to the Worm's serape that would eliminate that class from the world. The universities of the world had in class around of 150,000 students in medicine, and had some 50,000 doctors graduated and passing for an specialty which have been retired and had address to their homes to consider their situation of enterprise and the future of their carrier, and the way to make their lives in the future.

After those conversations, the president also send a diplomatic to Worm's houses asking for an appointment among him, the president of Canada, and the president of the United States, in order to analyze the world situation about the pharmaceuticals laboratories, and the medical class and the hospitals in the world, what would be the future that can wait all, because they would need medical assistance to have children, since all were giving birds over their own beds and without medical assistance, and only were needing some scissors to cut the umbilical cord.

Worm assisted to the meeting with pleasure to that meeting who had place around the airport international of the island among the presidents and himself, that meeting had good acceptation and much pleasure, due to the anxiety that the situation had produced because were too many millions that were in play, the profits of the pharmaceuticals alone the pills cost them 10 for 1 cent and used to sell them for around 1 dollar wholesale.

Is that the impact of the situation was much greater of all that everything they could say, it was affected the following ways: the pharmaceuticals, the sales detail the medicines, the nurses, the sales of medical supplies, the medical equipment, the laboratories pharmaceuticals, the paramedics, was too many aspects that were on diriment, only there was something that was for too much superior distance: the health of the people. And this pay for all.

The risk was to lose hundreds of billions at year, was something relevant, from be the richest more portentousness of the world would become to be the poor more poor unemployed that would be in the world, from posses the most sophisticated equipment in the world. Would pass to be the owners of a refrigerator for sale the bottles of serape. From make thousand of billions of dollars would pass to make a couple of hundred of dollars a month. What a great difference.

The meeting started with the blonde making a comment of the situation, and then the prime minister of Canada who was who ordered to the blonde that followed with his labor of investigate of purchase to Worm for his serape to put it to the drain it get something to the Canada or United States.

Later, after those, dissertations came the turn for the president of the island to take the word. This started saying that he gibe thanks to the God in heaven for have sent Worm to his country and that was a great joy for him to announce his turn for to addressed to so high potent as two of the seven great of the world and that him fell enlighten for having them as visitors in his country that he awaited they enjoy from the serape with apple and the other of grapes, that worm have had the chance of being from the plantation of around el Pedregal, and you will enjoy in a moment, the president of the Senate of the Unites States ask for a glass of water and was brought a lemonade, from the Worm plantation, which he took without protest for anything and then stand up to say that he wanted a glass of water but they served another think, what was that he got? And comment that a car that was bothering him was already cured, was that water or was something else, like serape what he got. Worm came to the speech to say:

Worm – the serape has a psychological effect in the mind of the people to take many times the flavor they want to receive, and as he wanted to drink water, it changes its flavor to simple water.

The delegates right away addressed to Worm in order to give then his comments about the future of the areas that worry them, and Worm named what was the world was before of the time of the pharmaceutical take control over the sickness of the world, comment with them over how the medical class was behaving in front of the sick people of the world how do they collect a lot of money for treat them clinically, how hospitals treat to the sick people hospitalized and how do they suffered each one of them, how were treated by the medical insurance, how were all bad treated and others lived a pleased life filled with abusive mistreat to the people in need, whom were sorry, he did not have pleased news for anyone of them.

The president of Canada ask him that if he were a representative of God on earth, how would be coming to us with this kind of abuse and inconsideration

with the world, how is possible that discriminate so strongly with sectors of the society that would can be against the sickness that he had been sending and had been finish them with their knowledge's and medicines formulated to satisfy to their sons. And the medical assistance, how the sickness how the nurses assistants, ambulances services offered, and all other attentions, why would stay on the road supporting needs and all others

Worm asks to them then:

Worm – Doctor, tell me, how much do you charge to someone who ask you how is cured a pain of a sore?

Doctor – I used to charge 100 dollars

Worm – Well, I will do that for free, and with some drinks of my serape that cost US$0.10 of a dollar get completely cured and foremost that foresheet them for any other future sickness for 10 hours and hold the sensation for thir for same price.

In the shortage, the meeting had been a defeat for the industrials, so they decided to withdrawals and start the military invasion of the island in a near future, no without to give them an ultimatum and challenge them as they use to of doing since always, them have not make themselves more skinny, or had show weakness in front of this critical situation that was presented were they were put between the sword and the wall, that situation was unacceptable for the more powerful countries of the world, that they have the capacity of destroy that island 70 times and could destroy them no matters they get allied with the rest of the poor world However they want to make it they will be defeated. What at a hell have believed those?

The countries of the United States of America and Canada, that had have the meeting with the president of the island and with the own Worm, have not been satisfied with the result, so that they start to talk with Germany, France and Russia, looking to form a good group to keep planning and if necessary to make the war unto them, unto that little island that with two shout well shout could be enough, or a good bomb well shut down to erase it from the map if necessary, that without to count the hidden asset that may have Mr. Worm which apparently look inoffensive at the entrance to the great powers that do not considered him dangerous at all, because his greatest assets were hidden.

The conversations with the greatest magnates will go slow according start the conversations, so their search for some associates that could be more aggressive, like Japan, China, Switzerland, Sweden Belgium, that beyond also produce medicines, and that necessarily put seem affected in a brief time.

On their side, Worm was not thinking anything, he was sat at the dining table, after had been enjoyed with his mother and brother a delicious family dinner. Were having their evening coffee while talking of the everything that had happened in those meetings, first with the blonde, that cause an scandal over the all country, followed for the pacification of the president paying to Vicente the bill that the blonde made, then the instant visit of the president of United States and Canada and for the president of the congress of the United States that no matter do not used to visit any country at all, had been interested for that meeting for the high industrial content, and the high volume that of interest that may affect, for example to the sector pharmaceutical, and sector medical national and international, sectors that represent trillions of dollars a month in their country alone.

The island was always a quite place to live, a place where never had to talk about assaults, steals, violence of any kind where there was not need to be watching the properties, or to be pending of anybody or nothing, and while more near the date, less desire hen either, were either was very much communication with out of the island where there was not hotels, when someone comes to visit were always to the house of someone in particular, nobody used to come as a curios, there was nothing to show, all that there was in the island was for the residents of it, no matter there were many places, that the people of the world would like one world to know places that there was not in anywhere in the world, because the Almighty God, had been done like that for that the people of the island do not desires to live it, and for they lived filled with love and happiness.

Always that comes a plain to the island, was full of people locals, because nobody from other place would come here, to visit us, or curious. One day arrived a plane full of weir people and that night result because pass the day and night going and coming looking where to sleep or eat, and they could not find any place, because as we said before, there was no places like that, the only place to spend the night it would be necessarily to be in your house or in the house of any neighbor, but that plain brought like 200 people that never had been there, and do not know anyone either, when the people of the island have gone to another country, they always stayed into hotels, and do not make friendship either, do not look conversation with any one either talk with any one, they look like emit, not because do not talk, but because they do not put any them of conversation to anyone, when going to an store, find what they want pay for it and go, or not to buy at all.

All the money exchange that was done in other countries, the currency was returned nor do mally next day, and all the banks buy it, as we know, the local peso was very desirable and respected because was back up with gold and diamonds yet, because it keep from contamination from the exterior. Its currency was under the constitutional back up of diamonds and gold, for all the paper money that circulated.

Now that this 200 people had arrive into the country, they were near to the capitol and the nation know for first time in its history, what is defined with violence, what is blood running by the floor, never in all the years that this world have since created, some like 5,500 years had been shown violence not the locals or foreign or the inhabitants knew what is to hit a noncitizen, here was a world of peace and friendship where weird time you go to visit some body, was to drink or eat, or maybe to have some kind of conversation of interest for you or for the other, the persons do not used to go as curious or to see how you are doing, but something needed.

There was no newspaper or magazines, no locals, or foreign that was not in use and the success or the news were received by TV or radio, they used to put music all they, and cut for news that was very well known, but now with those sirs do not know what would happen, they found some polices from the capitol by the market zone, where there were a lot of merchandise, and no matter it does not show up some little violence of any kind over there, always were watching the zone by the police, just in case, do not let became a chaos, but to stopped right there, the police were trained in personal defense and martial arts, and do not let themselves surprises, because were the only acts of violence that can be watch in the island. Cannot be seeing anywhere else neither they were doing acts of exhibition for that, but they live the uses, only the police used to practice those games, and over there were for life, when you get unto the list was a patriot act and were mostly for families completed and those families where dedicated to take care of the others.

Chapter 5

In the daily route for the center of the city, this group of patriot citizens have find with that group of weird been, because over there you could recognize a local for the way they dressed and the form of walk very particular, the clothe over there was done from the treads and the buttons and the all dress press was done locally, very different to the other places, in the world at sight the police ask directly: you should be those who came this morning in the plain. You should know by now, that there are no hotels here, or restaurant, and I doubt you have friends over here. The person who can lodge you live like 30 kilometers of distance in a town call El Pedregal, going southwest to go there need to take a route west, and go over there. The mother of the two young men is called Maria and the sons one is called Roberto and the other Worm, they are the only given to lodge people in this country, you should now you are the first people who come from a foreign country here.

The police Captain warn us that if we find you anywhere that inform you that with pleasure we facilitate campaign tents and latrines in the central park of the capital, to make a place to sleep with cushions, so you can be with some comfort, and the kitchen and others you can purchased in the hardware stores and the food in the locals supermarkets that you can find in all the towns, known that in this country, we do not use to apply violence, that we do not fight, but we will defend ourselves if attack, and you will go in the way you do violence, we will only deport you, to those whom do not behave in proper manners of care and affections.

We do not have laws, we are police but only watch so, there is no violence, we respect and make respect to the others, and that is it what we work, do not have jails because never ever break the peace, no matter that do not exist here. As you could now, nobody ever ask you to show a passport or to board our planes, or yours, behave yourselves correctly, so you can be an example, in that we can trust others to let them visit us, and maybe in the future we will have airlines coming and exiting this land, we do not have consular legations anywhere in the world, but that have change in the future. It depends on you. In the past some airlines had contact with us to open traffic with us, and we have tell them, that do not have sense or business convenience because we are weird persons we act like mountain people, and we really are, because our great cities are all in mountains, the flat surfaces are for agriculture only, there is no houses over there and nobody lives in the plantations because the not need to watch them when somebody is hungry, ask what they need and is given, we are given people, our use is to look for the gentle part on the others, not the violence.

Like in anywhere in the world we live here, they lived a vigilance of some 50 police officers to watch the 200 that have suggested to be together, do not enter by big groups into the stores, that do not provoke to the citizens, to asks for what their want, that do not try to do the thinks by themselves, here we try to help them as we can as friends like families, do not try to be foreign here, because that form do not work good.

The very same night, the police that are checking, fall asleep because they never have to watch anything so, they were not very pending of those sat in the park, talking and joking, and finally fall asleep, when the breaking of a window glass in a hardware store and a supermarket waken they up.

Fire people were running out of a hardware store with shovels, bowls, plates, forks, and other things, the polices stop them right away. First robbery in the history of the island, so there is another group living from the supermarket of the zone, a little group like 10 people were living with provisions from there to eat, because could not find what there are not, since the people do not used to buy provisions, they could not understand that way of life, but it was possible to purchase those thing for money.

The police did not know how to proceed in this case, since they did not have this situation before, and they are not oppose resistance, one of the police go and awake the captain who came in person immediately in a patrol, and impart instructions for get one of the buses of Worm to take them to the airport immediately. The plain that brought them was there waiting for them and would go with them to take them back to the place they came from, they never should come and will go this time at their first offense.

Captain – All that they try to take by force and hidden will be returned and paid to their respective owners, will robe to them, and nothing will take with them for their nasty attitude they will go with hunger and thirst and will pay for the damages totally, they will pay the door at the supermarket and a new crystal with the borders to de hardware store. Now, they will wait for their pilot at the airport, they will be jailed in the airplane. So they will depart at sunset.

They were complaining the visitors of the fault of hospitality of the country and the citizens, and that to they will present the complaint to the government as soon as they arrive there, and that never, ever will return to that place. It was said that nobody ever invite them to come, and if they would be behave as the locals, it would be able for them to stay for more time, that the government facilitated them the thing that were able for the foreign, like campaign houses, as there is no restaurants we open our homes for you to shared so you can have our food In our homes, nobody would let them with hungry, all were ready to share our food with them, or will collect any money for this service, but with placer and likely, had we serve them for free, only that no more than 4 per household, and only one time, next food would have to take place in with another family, cannot repeat in any house, or go to eat at any hour, they must present themselves at proper time and wait for the food to be prepared, because nobody would prepared for just in case, but after arrival.

The visitors realize that they had come to the paradise, and said that they were sorry, that it was an error they had committed, if they could forgive them for their fault, because this will not happen again, that in the future they will do by their for sand uses, and that they would like to stay for a longer time having joy with their friendship and partnership, if they would allowed them to stay for a week, and if they can get them to visit the places of interest, like the beaches, and beautiful places of the country.

Not completely they had finish saying all these words, the doors of the plain were open, the bus that was waiting had live to get a very great dinner and it was said, that they cannot live, that they have to feed well first to go, and a short time after the bus came with the food. The bus brought food for 500 of every kind in abundance of every kind, bread, plantains, casaba. Bananas, white rice, chicken with rice, cheese, butter, milk, fried eggs, eggs salcochados, scramble eggs meat, goat meat, and cover plates and the necessary equipment to eat, and there were extra for the locals that would like to join them, they brought also 500 seat and table for the same, they also had beer and cognac, rum for all, then musical agroupations of the country start to play music for the joy and for dance and after that, went to the place where they should sleep, and were playing more beyond the morning.

Next day, they were quiet completely, and the visitors sleep until noon, they did not want to wake they up, because the day before they had suffered a deception, so when they wake up a delegation of them went to the supermarket and the hardware store to ask pardon and say how sorry they were saying:

Foreign - That would never will be repeated, you are such good persons that do not deserve that we treat that way we treat you, and that they were very sorry for all that evil, that they do not thing they deserve that pardon that they had receive and their kindness on what they could imagine, going over they expectances even, they felt so happy for coming to that place, that they no more would like to go home, at that moment, if their invite they to stay, they would stay with them.

That night the president made himself present over there with a small commission and said, Anyone who wishes to stay, who want to live in peace and armory, have my permission to stay living here, but all that have violence in his heart, is going to be better to live, because there is no place for those heart here. Immediately the 200 went and filled the forms to stay, houses were assigned to them which had remain empty from the previous household that had died, the plain was dispatch empty, with no passengers, and was said to them, that they were nationals from now on, to stay sleeping there meanwhile the houses had been ready and delivered.

President - Participate from the welcome party that the all country offer to you, as a welcome to hour neighborhood, you will be all represented by the persons from the capital whom live in the center of the island, the all island will be in this party for the addition of 300 new members to our society, let see, give me a bottle of beer please, I want to be to open one.

And he drank it entirely from the bottle to the mouth, and when finished show a big smile sincere and a aaah! Of satisfaction for the happiness for the welcome to the new citizens and how delicious was the beer.

It had been installed a bit tent in place, for the reunion to eat the food. There were together and had ask permission to make a meeting with the door closed where they will choose a delegated to give thanks to the president and to the community for their hospitality, and that they have coming alone and lived their children minor of age, so they cannot stay very happy without them, as they should come those minor children which would be very happy to get educated in that environment that they have get to know by the good way and also at time to apply the force sp they behave correctly as advert before, and they fell all pleased.

Immediately after, the president ask for some cellular's phone and to put them on line and call their sons for them to go to the airport, and planes send by the island go in the morning to pick them up, so they can be waiting over there until pick up in each airport where they could be awaiting and any other person who wishes to come to live with love and peace that come with them, the country will make a party with them, that come to work and live with happiness, the island await to them all who want to come, maybe this invitation will not be available in the future, but it is now available.

New houses were build for the 200, and they decided to build hotels, restaurants, and the local have joy, they had not enjoy the majority and of what was to leave the daily routine of eat of what other use to cook for them in the restaurants, they had lines of kilometers to eat out of their own home, many of them, go and hosts in hotels that were build the reservations was needed to make with over a year in advance, always were full, when a room occurred any damages it was necessity to fix it immediately because always there is someone, from those parties that the president gave and its opening, was in the island great happiness, was make like a national party with 3 days of national party in the country, the only national days besides the days for the Lord from heaven the God of the sky and earth.

In the days of Saturdays the people do not go to work at all, it was a national day dedicated to the Lord and their rest, nobody had the occurrence of work in those days, if to someone present a need that could not poster gate it need to apply to a neighbor. There was so much harmony in the country including the new 200+, they were example for all, lesson learned in its first time there I invite you like the nationals in this story used to lived and how live all together now, so never again they caused any trouble, it was a lesson learned at once, and the forgive that receive, I invite you to be perfect in front of God and have hin as the witness.

There was not in the island any church, or temples at all to adore the God most high, but the meetings were done in the parks, every Saturday were celebrate those meetings, in every year that the island existed it never rain in that day, the Lord let go the rain from that day and reward them until with those details, as they do not have roof on the Saturday, he did not let then wet either, one day that fall a little rain on Saturday, nobody occurred to go home, but they stayed there, until the day finished, and that rain fall on top, refreshing they a little more from the fresh that was the day, never they did need air conditioning over there in the country, with the sole exception of Worm who was always hot, the rest never considering it as necessary because the temperature was always agreeably day and night.

By those days everything was happiness in the town and Worm ask what happened what was the reason for all that he was seeing so much happiness and drinks, were open more and more bottles, more bottles than those he had seen opened during his all life. What was the reason for those celebrations, and Roberto tell him, is that you do not know the latest happened in the capitol? Have come a plain full of tourists, and did not find how to spend the night, the government through the police install for then tents , they robe in the supermarket and in a hardware store, and now have stay to live here in the island, they have plans to build hotels, and restaurants and everything else the country is changing quickly have lived a plain the one who brought them to pick their children's to the different airports where they will be awaiting to be pickup there are like 100 children in total that would to come, it has made a houses building for the future couples that would get marriage, I am telling you that this is a revolution that is in form, you should be having a drink and celebrate also.

Worm - That is not a problem, let me have it, please give me one from that refrigerator, and take one for you too Roberto, tell me what had said mama from this, what do her is thinking about that?

Roberto — Well, I thing she does not know anything yet, she hear the news at ten o'clock, and now is when are about to start the transmission.

Worm – Turn on the radio to hear the news, to find out the official news about that, looks very interesting.

Roberto connect with the news at 10:00 ad come the communicator and say: Here Dario Montas transmitting the 10:00 news, last night had happen sensational, here sirs, have come an airplane with 200 tourist, something never seen in the island, it never had come anybody like tourist to this island in the all history, and instructions were given to them, but bi night, lucks like they forgot what is was, and broke a glass to the hardware store and broke a door to the supermarket Navidad, and robe bowls and all the utensils for cook food, and uncork food also, and were surprised by the police that were asleep, while watching, and wake up because of some noise they made, due they did not find any place where to get cooked food, neither nock the doors of the neighbors anywhere, so, the police did their work and for the first time catch some fishes out of the water.

After of pay for the damages and the product of their work, and repair the damages, living the premises in the condition there were before start the breaking, were transported to the airport, came the president to say goodbye, when one of them ask for a pardon, and let them to stay for a week longer, that it was the time they intent to stay in the island, because they finally had discovery how good they live over there, or would like to stay living there, if allowed, but they did not expect him to please them after what they did, but if allowed they would stay, because they were living the way it was describe in the Bible, when you start reading it.

The president then, gave permission for them to stay, filled out the necessary papers and all were subscripts to the naturalization, since there is no immigration in the island so, it was necessary to declare them sons of the country and right away were documented and are all of them now national citizens, and a diner was celebrated the most wide diner celebrated in the island since all time, a revolution of feast was next day, better said today, we are still celebrating everywhere as a day of happiness, a day of celebration and forgiveness and peace, happiness is everywhere, it provide motive for celebrate, in all the possible side.

The truth Worm is that if we do not close the warehouse, soon the people is going to come with the police to enforce us to go to celebrate, and I think it would be very good go to the capitol but already. Well say the employees that put several cases of serape of different kinds in the trucks and lets go, each one in its truck for the capitol, and celebrate in great scale. I will pass to pick up mama, so she go with me, and celebrate this happening.

After this commercial pause, here, Dario Montas continue with the news. A real revolution have been form, the president have give the empty houses that were empty because some persons were died and those houses have not been assigned for other new citizens to live and those are decided to build attachment to those, as well as hotels, restaurants and all the commodities of a modern country, and after listen to those declarations, the celebration had been even higher than it was before, the musicians, have been playing their instruments since yesterday, without stop, playing and drinking beer, with a great happiness, this is a enormous proportions party and I am sure that Worm support this and will bring his serape for to continue this, and yes, there is him arriving with his bother Roberto, had coming each one in his trucks, let's see now if I come appointed with the aspect of the serapes.

There are them discharging them, and continue the party, now with more health and more power , how good is to live in this island, the president has call the mayor of this zone that will come to celebrate with the citizens new and old and their sons that are coming flying and that will land by 4:00 o'clock in this afternoon that will add 300 new citizens extra to the population of the island, so they will need 100 new houses to live, and are saying that will make attachments to them to celebrate continues dinner with their neighbors, to have even more happiness, so they will share dinner if possible in a daily manner, and exchanging from one house to another, but for them to be together if possible every day, their happiness is so great, that they need to share it with the neighbors, from today and forever.

It looks like the live here will be even better than ever, because these citizens are much better than the locals, they share with us our good habits and are bringing to us they are unite to our good things, and are making that even better than ever, so they want also that their sons go to school with perfect attendance, and even work after school and study during the night for next school day, and do not complain, nobody in the country is unemployed and there is no jails or delinquents, either there are written laws, there is no senators or representatives, and are not even required, that is qualified like a perfect society where to live in, that we do accept visitors, but we ask to nobody that come, no for tourists, but if somebody finally come as a tourist, to find lodge, no matter do not like that better than our homes.

We should remember that Worm in his 15th birthday was an arm trafiquing, but nobody could ever provide a proof of he does that, and who sold hundreds of thousands of rifles, pistols several millions of bullets shells rifles, pistols several millions of shells mortars, up to 4 tanks of war, sold to the country of the civil war that we do not want to mention hear, and is been retired from that activity, and has become an enormous producer of medicine and refreshments for our country and also for the world that the product of Worm is the only one industrial for export of the island, and that is enough for to purchase all that expend inside that is produced in another country.

Is that the happiness that is going overboard the parameters of it, and is a enormous happiness that we all fell from inside from inside our heart, that those persons that tried of make us damage, did not desired really, but because of their habits, tried to resolve the need that is was presented because of their fault of affection but at realize the kind of life that he has when you realize when you deliver yourselves to the others, discover the paradise of heaven, and with the serape of Worn, there is no sickness, discover the perfect life.

The news for today, say our producer that will stay open for that our co citizens keep informed, and how is a great news on what we are passing today, there is no need of suspend anything, and sirs. We are informed that the plain with the children's just landed with the children's had just land in the airport of the capitol, and the fathers had just live for over there to pick them up and bring them to their respective homes, that had been furnished and prepared for life in the way that they are decided to lived, we has been informed besides that each one of the houses were prepared to live with a dining table for 40 seats each one, because they desires have comfortable seated the neighbors that they will have invited to dine with them every night and the neighbors that will have invited to dine every night, and the neighbors are also building attachments, because they desire to return the favor for that do not be very tired because of that. And that there is a great happiness in doing that shared then in using them, in that way they will have harmony for all, that a calendar is been prepared, mean willed, while the male work in the tables, the woman work in the calendar of in what house is going to eat each day.

But hey, is coming Mr. Rupert the English Sir that have come to retired himself from active life and to live his last years with us, had not desires to lose this celebration, have come and there it is, behind of the Roberto's truck pulling out one of the cases of syrup of strawberry, has put it on the ground and pull one of the bottles of plastic, and is and is drinking directly from one of the bottles of strawberry, ah, wow delicious should be feel that, and is coming with one bottle to me, I hope that is bringing it for me that I like so much, I hope is for me, he is bringing it for me, soon will be enjoying it wait a minute, listeners, this is too exciting, this is too good, as for keep talking straight, I have to drink now from this serape, that among all is my favorite.

Chapter 6

Since today, there will be a celebration in all houses of our country, is permitted show up in any house to eat with them and there is not going to be reason to offended, and if the food is not enough, go and get some more to a neighbor's house, but that should not be a reason for to stop the celebration, if you do not have what to cook that day, go and pick up something to a neighbor's house, but not to stop the celebration, that nobody let see how much cost or what to cook, because the meaning and main reason is the celebration, not how to celebrate, lets share on what everyone have available.

With all the preparation of the new human way and family union in the country, we are sure that the life sill be a lot more overtake and we will have more comfort, imagine, that now in place of cook in your house all afternoon, will cook one day, and will eat in other houses six days, plus the environment of feast in which will be eaten every one of the dinners, will be nights of feast every night, will not be this a better way of life.

On the other hand, Miss Mary is of feast, there is nothing that she feel better than this relations among neighbors that are kind of family meeting of realize about the problems and torments and will shared then with the neighbors and we will share with them, and solve among us, as a big family, all our problems will start from there to be share ones, and they will convert in little ones, since they are shared, they are not going to be mine, but ours, beside that as we will see to come, we will be better prepared to receive them when they want to surprise us.

The farmers keep planting the land, and the president have giving instructions to the department of agriculture that make an actualization for the distribution of the need of feeding that will be with the new modality, as also for the new 300 members that we will have, and also with the groups that are forming to share the food that will make more efficient the distribution of the agriculture.

We will remember that the blonde when he left, and the presidents, came out very dislikes and promised that conversation will not finish there, but that they will continue until they get diversified its medicinal program and their medical system. The president had designed Worm for to continue these conversations for which this is getting prepared to make a trip to Germany and to the United States, to pacify this relationship.

At arrive him to Germany is receipt at the airport buy the minister of Industry and for the minister of health, which feels impatient before the great treating that their procedure means for their powerful and medical, what is a potency overwhelming worldwide and that it is see as a menacing, to be diminished until the floor, in the graphic design of the growing or decreasing of the level of the productive sector, which keep them very worry.

Worn participate them that the partial solution would be that do not purchase their famous serape, and that keep the poisoning as always had been doing, that their country had lived always without serape, the popularity and the over sale that have had lately is due to sincerity and acceptation of the people that if they desire and the money is for then that important, to stop of use it, and suppressed to their people, and the accepting of the people, that if they desire, and the money for them is so important, that stop of using it and suppressed to the people from drinking fruit juice with cocaine, front to drink poison, If that is the relation they desire to make to decide what is good or what is bad for their people.

Once this friendly arrangement was made of that will leave of to purchase the serape that Gusano manufactured, and that them will buy the medicine quemicals necessary all will come back to normal think. Gusano then, decided go to the airport for to return to his country, or maybe go to visit to the government of the United States, in order to find any intermediate point of peace and harmony.

So, he speak over the phone with the president of his country, and this say to him, that address himself directly into this United States, where he has a reception committee for to treat this theme, that are very worry ad how good that it to be you the one who represent the government for to talk with them, because you are the one that justly manufacture the serape that has generated all this matter.

Right away, give instruction to the pilot for to take him into the United States, particularly to the District of Columbia, where are awaiting in the same airport, a little commission, but with all the support of the central government for to negotiate the matter with that theme, that they want syrup, but that they cannot stop from buy it, because it was an diplomatic arrangement and a king of proof, in order to verify, that there was a causality of that syrup that cure all the dolencies, and that prevent new sickness, and to prevent from new sickness, not only bacteria's, or microbars, but also over hurt and hurt in bones, that the bad that had was that all the prognostics have result true, and that the applications of them were good.

At arriving, immediately they got involved in a conversation directed to solve the conflict, the fist that they enforced was that offer them a glass of that delicious drink, and he please him immediately, in a minute were all drinking of that drink, served with ice to better pleasure, and offer the same treat than Germany, no obligation to purchase and effective drink, and continue to produce their chemical medicine for their inhabitants , and for the rest of the world that would decide to purchase to the, whatever they may need.

United States immediately made the exigencies for to diminish the production of the sweet liquid, for that could be peace, because the people that manufacture those medicines, were powerful, and do not were ready to get covered.

The commentaries that were in conversations with the countries of Europe and Japan besides and that will make the war if they do not allow overcome, that those were special conditions that they were imposing.

Worm communicate them, that he was on a visit there, for a commission that the president of his country had comissionate, that he is a encomendated by his president, that he is a man of respect for the superior orders of the others to him that it was not his decision, nor his labor exclusive, but the de wishes of his government that wishes to have a peaceful relationship with the inhabitants of his country, but the all country is offering passports to his citizens and visas to the foreign to maintain diplomatic relations opened, relations those that only give favor to the other countries because with their visits, only can bring us troubles, more than solutions, and nothing good we are going to take out, not even devises, because on what their countries, because on what your country import is really minimum, and that always had export more than that has import, because from Agricola products and mines for example, are exclusives in the world and all the others need acquire over there, while that his country import vehicles of motor, need only two planes for overfly the island on a military form, and other as for passengers, now as the country is opening itself to the world, started with airlines that opened the travel airlines to operate the rest of the world, besides tourists ships, for they can bring our nationals from another countries and take ours with yours.

Then, after these words were finished this meeting, where the American minister communicated that since that moment is suspended the imports of his famous drink, but do not forget of him, that him would like a lot and would like to continue enjoy some cases a month, or could make an importation for a all year if the product keep if keep good for all that time.

Worm – This smiled and said softly as of him used to talk, of course, of course yes.

As Worm return to his country immediately got an interview with the president and communicate, that as much as Germany as the United States would stop for import the juice, so as those novelties look like their interest and the attention to the money weigh more that their interest and attention in the money weigh more than the good health with more than the good health of the people, and that to be prepared because later or earlier they will attack with the army, and to this would be tremendous, that if the juice could make this damaged, the war inequal would do would be more damaged.

This is the marc that Gusmani have with the rest of the world, internal peace and war with the exterior, now we have that the exterior is interning in it and this is something that the foreign should consider before to shut its destructor fire, because this island do not desire to kill or hurt to another, but to cure them and address them for the way that is agreeable to the human and to the divine, to the natural and to the over natural.

Worm then have the idea go to make a visit to his aunt, sister of his mother, in order to put her in alert of the what she can expect of what may come to their country for the happenings and the reaction before the fruit of his serape and how the powerful countries of the world have been interrelating that change the divine things for the mundane that do not put an effort in the details that really have valor, but in the aerial that have poor value.

When the aunt see him in the stairs to the mountain of her house right away call two servants for they to go and help him with the packages with those he always come to the house of his dear aunt, that really is his truly mother, because it was her who give birth to him and have pass in front to the all country as it was Mary, what happened is that they are twin sisters and substitute to Mary in her house when she was pregnant of Worm, she went to the hill and the child stayed in the city at care of her aunt, but nobody realize nothing of that, not even the child, this was a secret between the two sisters.

It was not now the moment for that Worm knows yet, but that this expected that have a security more extreme, a real need in the country and yet have not arrived yet, but it seem to come, it seems to be its moment

At arrive home, the aunt save for him a special food and gave to him to drink of her special drink, took him to seat in the kiosk they have in front of the house, with a wide view of the valley and the garden, until the sea that shower the capitol, that special view, the hill was very high no matter it was move in car almost the all way, it was necessary to walk the last meters that make themselves very tired, inclusive for a strong and young man like Worm, because that last part was very lean in the hill, but that was the part means that it will last a little to be surrounded for all her love, his mother said to him that if a present situation, she and Robert will come to refuge in her caress and affections.

No matter she knew that she was not a problems lover but that she likes no matter she has something to sacrifice, that have peace and love for everywhere, always peace, first at the middle and at the end. That those caves that she knows that they are that were at the hill and to count for a extreme security for them where was reserved for the moment more angus, either they would like to uses them, because that means that they were at war, and this could destroy the all island, that she knew what she was saved in the hole that opened when those rays in that occasion behind for more than 23 years, before of the Sir that both of them knows is gone and never return.

For this reason, Miss Mary had never returned to the hills of rosebud. Because were awaiting those remembered moments from their old lost love, when both sisters fall in deep love from the same man, and he had has to both of them, and to each of them he put a child in hers womb, a son and heir, to aunt Rupert he deposited Worm and to Miss Mary Roberto, and they have agreed that Miss Mary educated to both of them, so they lived together as the two brothers anyway they were, and to both woman the father had love in extreme much.

Worm stayed by two weeks with his aunt, who he love as she was his real mother, and then returned to the house of his mother Maria, in order to continue with the direction of his business, the country of the Caribbean to whom Worm before used to sell arms, was asking him that return to the business, because was in a desperate situation to which Worm said to no will do that, but instead it will very much more convenient, that he has the solution for them for their conflict on a very different way, that securely they would like much more because we're on a very pacific way, that that would fix as is describe in Armageddon, but to the way of a strong worm.

They did not understand these words, so they left the conversation for another moment, in shortcut, at the end Worm told them that they will not have to shut any more shut, but all would be friendship and armory with a lot of comprehension in the future, that trust him, that he knows the ways to solve the think on the most convenient way for the better, that in the future, that trust him, that he knows the ways for to solve the thinks on a more convenient ways to solve the thinks on a more convenient way for all, that relax and have a little of patience, because it may last a couple of months.

Worm got down and was reunited for lunch with Miss Mary, then continue his way for the warehouse, first went to the greenhouse where all was working very well, each one already knew how to do their work, and all used to do it In the best of their ability, all the process was automatic, where the personal only have to turn on the machinery and then to be watching that nothing to make a disorder but to continue duly, and if something get out of place, the personal fixed immediately, for not to produce important losses.

Once confirmed what was to wait, followed the way to the warehouse that was from where he used to dispatch the orders of purchase of merchandise to the all world, that the island has acquired already two ships and tree planes in order to dispatch all that they sell internationally to the all world, and for all the country have 150 trucks, in that way looking to this way looking to this, the business of the serape was an empire already, had grown and was solid enough that do not need of his presence, but Robert and Miss Mary could handle it in detail, because the 200 new residents work there with them and were persons very dedicated and hard workers. In the new farm that had purchase Worm, there was springs, from which pure water were get a very pure water, that do not need a big process of purification for to prepare that enormous quantity of serape to distribute worldwide, a big donation was made to the poor people of the world, for example to the people of Africa and Indonesia, trailers were send with no cost whatsoever, not even the fleet was charged, and several times at year, for they had enough so they have enough and could be in good health year round.

Worn then addressed to the dominoes club where started a competition between him and a friend, against two partners of the club, and decided to make that competition as he said, to see which one was more sharp in the game, because he already knew what was better, or play more appropriate, because always, win one and one in all their confrontations they always finished tided, but they had a very good time, excellent moments sharing with that very entertained game. Never was Worm a very good sporty man that is why he was playing to the dominoes, either could learn to play music.

Playing the dominoes, it was late and Miss Mary was awaiting him for dinner, because the dinner will had place in her house and everything was ready, only him was missing and two of the neighbors, everything else was ready, and Miss Mary botters a lot that people come late to her table, more than Worm used to be on time and uses to take a shower before dinner.

That night there was an special invited to dinner that her mother had invited, it was sergeant Berta, the very beautiful sergeant, that was help that had help so much when the problem of the 200 and their situation in from of the park in the capitol when they were installed to spend those nights. Since they see each other both delivered in a saw directly into the eyes and extend a wide smiley how if they was treated every day, with the same treat, the same treat, in that sight they let to know each other the attraction that there was from one to another, and from her to him, as if would be promising eternal love, but it was a delivery of affection of mutual love abundant.

It came a neighbor from the warehouse of Worm, and ask to him why he felt always with high moral and always was dedicated to do the good to the others, and Worm answer: because a lot of people looking to change the world, according I have read, and I do not intent to changed, I only search to make it a better world, not only a different one because the people denied in from of the change, this is something that everybody accept and let it be without a bad feeling, not so to the changes that comes only to interrupt the uses of the people, is different when you know that something is better than another.

So where the thinks with Worm, because he was better everyday more, because all on what he does move in turn to a better quality life, because since the day that was born, until today all had change for the better, and not only with the simple purpose of a change, because he was a good man and because his ideas are for the welfare with better quality life, so was the serape and so it was with what he was working in the new construction behind of the greenhouse and for what he was purchasing the new farm where he make a plantation for salads, besides there was were where the plant of fabrication of the serape, due to the good water facilities of water funds that there was that move in a system similar to the one of the Great

Lakes situated in the border between the United States and Canada that feed enormous water founds, for example from Lake Erie to the lake Ontario, that there is a little geographic unlevel and is taken as use form mother nature the Niagara river, and in the pass to form the Niagara falls who were form for the different materials from the underground, part build of rocks, solid rock, and part softer than the other. The rocky part stayed inert on top, and the soft part, was moved and went with the water, and was move with the water down river, and with than unlevel was form the falls with the time. With that effect was form one of the most beautiful paradise in the all world with an unlevel for more than 100 meters high and keep growing, the water canal that continue covering the uneven ground cover a man at sight I can say like 5 times, with a water movement as 150 yards wide at sight, so we are talking of much, very much water.

The United States do not offer a treat in vane if they are not planning to do something they do not say any menace, so, when they say, they accomplishing is for that have been in conversation with the powerful, for when attack to have a back up at least economical, and is have been some time they have been planning how to revenge of those poor persons and have already to England, France, Canada, and Germany eating on their plate, need yet Italy, Japan, and Russia that fight always on their side, because both are property from the same man and actual king of the world behind scenes, no matter they had no communicate anything yet, they now, they have eating in their side at all time, they have a public image of contrary, but dip are from the same team for the exposed before.

Our people do not know from all that is happening behind the scenes, in good English and betrayed. And hidden as it was his style, not even the press has realize of what been realize, the office of press have not emit none idea of doing any action, so, that there is no way of inform of this that could be something substantially important for one or for other because you attack all old peace of wood and come out tremendous poisonous scorpion one of those that do not cause damage.

In the island we are trusted that we have peace, and we would have and we will keep having it, because we act correctly, we do not wish the bad for any person, national or foreign, so we act well for that we all get going well on this way, that either need to wait for the others want or have interest in do to us any bad, this is the secret of Costa Rica, for example, as do not have any army, cannot wait that another country that yes have it, would want to make any invasion, because the all rest of the world would see this with very bad taste, maybe like an abuse, with a lot of dislike, is like pull rocks for the smaller than you, and that is something unforgettable and intolerable.

Anyway, come to the presidential palace a notice of what the United States are planning an military attack to any small country, because they have their float of assault for small military movement, so, the island that is the country they are involve in military questions and conflict, is whom should be alert, said the press note that arrived to the president hands just this morning for which has been put in alert to the marine and the air force, which are in watch of the communications and radial signals and others, such of the communications, radio signals and others, such to the watch of the ships in patrol that have the marine everywhere.

A cloudy day, at dawn, the Marine of the island alert that is watching a patrol with several big boats of war that are approaching to the coast of the capitol of the country, for which recommend watching extreme and maximum alert, because this could mean maybe they may have the intention of invade the island, that nothing friendly could mean this, the friendly used to come by airports never by water, by over there come those which need heavy military arms, no light diplomatic equipment.

Right away, the air force, with their only plain of vigilance or attack, is watching to the fleet that is approaching to moderated speed, and that is not taking us by surprise for anything, because of the news that we receive before have us alert and in watching constantly, because advised war will not kill the soldier, or will hurt without advise.

The news by radio or TV start to exit and the people already start and the people is starting to realize that the serape is working in the opposite direction, in place of save us, is attacking us, and possibly hurt us reply, then the people that before was Worn as a hero, start to take him as a mortal enemy, the people do not want to drink the delicious serape, that before was an national pride, now is had been changed to worldwide enemy, the cartels that were proclaiming him for mayor or any other political position hi may desire are been getting dirty with old used motor oil, with used cooking oil and any other thing that dislike the people but nature refuses his truck this morning with urine and fecal pieces deposited on top, the island is not that place of peace, where the people used to live in a friendship and family union that were the envy for the all world, at least for the rest of it, now their world is looking at the inverse sense, and this is for only a treat.

The fleet places the anchor like 5 nautical miles from the coast of the capital and sends a bullet of the canon that fall in the center of the park, without cause lesions to any person but damaging seriously a gloried in the center of the park. Here is the reason for this visit what did they come to, and this bullet talk by itself, and it has said that they have the intention of attack and destroy the country completely, seeking only or mainly the plantations of Worm because affect seriously to the abusive rich and abusive of the poor people.

A boat of invasion is approaching to the coast and it looks like is coming in it a military of hi rank, is informed in the news that is an admiral of the marine who is coming in it, and possible desire a preliminary conversation before to take any military action beyond what they have done, before they cause future damages to the country, taking into consideration that the island do not have any marine, air force, or military forces how to defend themselves, or desire to have it, they cannot even thing in confronting with the United States, the more powerful country in the all world in military language or any other similar language that do not be friendly.

The admiral of the marine from North America, address himself to the palace of the president, not yet in a military mission, but yet in the diplomatic, surely will deliver to the president an ultimatum address by a league of rich nations against one of the more poor that have dear to attack to one of the more powerful industries of the world oligarch and now it came directly over the incipient industry of Worm that is in danger, the ultimatum say that:

Communicate to the island of Gusmani:

It is communicated that starting now, you have one day time for to destroy the plantations and to stop the manufacture the famous serape made to cure the people of the world from all sickness of the world, since you do not obey to this terminal communicated, the country will be annihilated and destroyed everywhere, will not stay stand not even one sole house that will not to be desapeared.

Signed by

The United States o America, Canada, Germany, France Italy England and Japan.

Please answer to this communicated before 6 o clock of the morning of tomorrow, if we do not receive any answer before that time, we will consider the answer as negative answer and will proceed to the attack immediately, because this situation is intolerable no matter our countries have prohibit the entrance of that merchandise by our ports, for consider it a tentative to the health of the people, it has been entered as smuggler of fruit juice camouflaged in people baggage , but we now that the health of the people is in jeopardy, also we have receive imports of that merchandise in sending of concentrated juice from Brazil and others countries, our analysis have confirmed that, so we have considered the only way safe will be destroying the plantations so, it does not come to produce again.

Before this communicated. That have been transmitted to the world press, the all world is irritated and the rich countries, are been seem now as enemies of the world and brutal prosecutors of the commonwealth upon which they have been doing as brutal prosecutes of the good will, and from the thing, they had done scaring and shame, because have been anchoring their military ships in front of the port of the capital because and also near the capital of all of the countries more populated or the world: four airplane carriers in front of the cost of China, 2 airplane carriers in from of India and two in front of the coast of Africa, all loaded with planes modified for use of prosecuted and bombers, modified for the double purpose

While all those maniobras were prepared the president was reunited with his government team looking for alternate solutions, the island was converting in the most visited, we will remember that the 200 were build hotels for the nationals in the main beaches of the country and one in the main cities where used to come the visitors that familiars or people very sick, that they believe more in the serape of Worm that in the quemicals preparation from the super powerful.

Those measures of the populations of the world irritated too much to the government of the rich countries, who had act as they used to, insulting. Passing over them, pushing killing to everyone that put in the way with the end of defy its authority. This was something intolerable that they never ever will accept or will tolerate.

At this point, all looks like that the war is inevitable, and that destruction of this country is already a fact, the only is that the rich in its avalanche destructive, have forget of one detail, who is that they are defiant? To a country? To a man? Or is against the humanity or against another power that do not have powder or gunpowder? That doesn't have not ship or plain? In that the island has any defense, the government has taken this thing as national or something general, is the product of a man what have caused all this revolt, and not even have taken this measures of defense, we look like that this is similar to any topic of the old history?

Do we remember the story of king Nebuchadnezzar? The king that the God from heaven who considered himself the most powerful of the world, with all that power with all that power and was sent to eat herb for 7 years, that take shower with the rain that fall from heaven? Is for that, which we should humble and leave us of all that importance that in the long term turn against ourselves, and never finished well those which work like that.

Worn was in his office of the warehouse mediating, and considering the situation, also thinking if the president and his team of people where thinking and evaluating the factors duly because this was not a situation of easy solution, friendly of easy, this has to resolve with power, no matter it be psychological power, maybe not which shooting, or blood no matter it be only the psychological one that was the really important for him, it has not speaking too much about the details that gave its origin to Worm, and why that name? Because to an important is put a name of one of the insect more despicable of the world? Of course, that this is only a story, but could be for real? All that come into the imagination could make it for real, right? I am sorry maybe I wake you up, but hold on and get your concentration again for you enjoy more.

Soon we will enter in the origins of Worm, you will understand that it was necessary to present it him this way, on another form it would be too cold, it was necessary this. Well, Worm is being not taking into account, when always was him who resolved the important problems of the nation, would be doing the role of Daniel hear? The man that Nebuchadnezzar either used to take into account but when other used to put him into his mind and his memory?

The president and his equipment of work still looking for solutions for the conflict that in order to solve this situation, they understand that if they please to the invaders and they say yes, and do it, the country will be condemn to the misery, because it already had costume rely to the good things and expensive, with the enormous affluence of devises that is having the country now with the serape, it will be bankruptcy literally monetary and commercial, besides of the enormous situation of good health that it had overcome fruit of this drink that also is medicinal and fruit of a war, due to the importance worldwide that it has come to have. But who is who have initiated this and complete goodness? One? Or someone that is in the meeting of the team of the government? Or one that not even form part from a commission or would it be some one that only is taking into consideration only to ignore?

Miss Mary who is been away from all this movement of question of the day, turn on the radio and the channel 24 hours at the day, do a recount of the happenings that have repeat already like 6 times, but due to the importance, do it by 7th times. Already are 4pm and the ship arrived like by 7 o' clock in the morning to the place where they are now, inert by complete. Because it has receipt orders from the admiral, of not to take orders of the admiral for not to take any military action until he is on board of the ship, no order from him, unless it come from someone with a higher rank than him, but not to take any order from him from outside of the ship.

The presidential team is still reunited yet, with no press realize, or communication with the exterior from the salon, nobody enter or exit over there, they had not taken lunch and is have given order of do not get any food or make it, until any idea to be fruitful or that bring light to a good solution, but in all that time nobody come out with something satisfactory, the admiral, conscientious of that is not something easy what he had bring until there is this day, it is quiet in the bar of the town, center of the city capitol, having joyful with the fruit of the discord, because while all go from that way, he had already drank two gallons from the serape and the partners of the bar, laugh from his attitude, one of them very sharp tell him:

Roberto – Admiral, are you personally making on us and have you come to our only bar to insult us, drinking you on what have you been ordered to destroyed?

The admiral stand up, remove his had from his head and say:

Admiral – You have all right in the world, but I want you to know, that I am not happy of accomplish this absurd order and to trample carrier autodestruccion, because to destroy this, it would be like to destroy ourselves a little, because it would kill the only opportunity that have the humanity of can cure if some mortal sickness overcome, and I am conscientious of that, because many books of medicine I have read, searching for a cure for a sickness that had my wife and mother of my children's, and the only cure I could find was this divine juice, that had come to be the return of my own goodness, of my children and my wife. That is why I am here, sharing with you all, divine town from God, because I am feel to be an assessing, and at the same time a suicide.

Chapter 7

Admiral – The sensation of refreshes is centered in that someone get full of violence, and take an firearm and shoot me into the head or the brain, and kill me. I had receive news that a few years ago that in this country there is a being, a mobster that is a trafiquer of fire arms that have maintain the war or guerrilla in one of the countries from central America. Not would have that person an arm and I had he in centered take revenge on my me, and murdered me? Roberto says to him.

Roberto – Come with me, I will put to talk with him, with that mobster, because now on day is no more than the patriot that most had defended his country in the all life, in the 20 years that today accomplish, they had close the doors of his business because is after six, and you will come with com with me, I am inviting myself to have dinner in his house today, and you will come with me, Roberto, to eat in the Mafioso's house.

Admiral – But I . . .

Roberto interrupts and tells to him

Roberto – You nothing admiral, you are a visitor in our country, and will be a visitor in our house today, because you have been announced already with our mother, my name is Roberto, brother of the mobster, who is the inventor of the serape that save the life of your wife.

At arrive to Miss Mary, mother of Roberto and of Worm, the admiral fell small, when he saw that a being so patented that was who prevail the all need of devise for the all country, would live in a humble house, and that invite to dinner to persons of so low economical level, when because his activities he should be the richest man in the all country.

So, he considered a great privilege to present himself before his presence, brother and mother, besides it should be there sat at his table some 10 compatriot of him, part of the 200 from the scandal form a few months ago, when the serape was launch recently to the international market, at coming there on hands of Roberto, right away was invited to have a seat at the table to have his dinner, that the proper night had nothing special, no matter it be his birthday; they were having casaba, green bananas, chicken, cheese, butter made of milk of cow.

Worm – Is a great honor for my family so humble to receive in our home to an officer of so high rank, that could not imagine, that would be motivation for him to include us in his itinerary.

Admiral – Nothing of itinerary, this visit was purely casual, and if you have some food for him it would be an honor for me, it would be a great honor, and that have receive it with pleasure, because have not eat nothing for the all day, that he could eat nothing during the all day, and had a hungry that hi could eat a horse with the all tail.

Miss Mary – That would be a terrible problem, because we do not have horse in the island, but I can order to cook a cow complete, including the defecation. If you need to, then, he says:

Admiral – The only think is that could last too long, and for then I will have so much suffering, and this was a visit due to Roberto, who had brought him to the house of the mobster that would help him to finish with his life.

Worm – If you drank from the serape in the quantity that Roberto say, that would make you immortal for a few hours, so, there was nothing that I could make to help you to accomplish with your objective. I am asking myself why you need to mention those nasty words in my house, what think was bothering so much for that?

Admiral – He repeat the story of his wife, and as the serape cure her totally from her sickness and as he was the emissary of destruction for that which had been for that much welfare for him and family.

Worm –There is nothing in the world who can destroy that, who had made so much good to the world, and you presence here is no casual, but programmatic, so, relax and have you dinner quite, because you would never will be responsible of the what happened from now on with the ship that brought you here none the big nor the small the one you use to come to the coast, because you will not return there, your wife and children are in the airport already and will come to the island in the first plane in the morning, the chauffer of the warehouse will pick up her and the children and will join with you in the mountain.

They ate dinner, all joint, and then a coffee was prepared that they drink in the gallery of the house, while they sang a family song with a lot of happiness and the satisfaction that was natural in that house, also in the all country. The emotion again embargo Worm only the idea of to know that would be with his mother, his real mother, the woman that brought him into this world, because Miss Mary was in reality his aunt, who had make him grow to him and so fine way to him educated.

Worm invited the admiral to a ride by the town, and took him for a walk by the beach where took a cold beer and had a long conversation over what it could happen.

Admiral – The navy float that brought him here, in order to accomplish his mission, probably will destroy the island completely, when down comes, those were his orders and nothing will stopped his tripulation from that.

Then Worm took the admiral to the balcony of the bar and asks him:

Worm – Here we have a view of the bay, look here, in that direction is the capital, only like 20 km of distance and over land, and over ocean from this elevated we can see 30 km, is not that sir? Now, tell me where is your fleet?

Admiral – Do you see that harbor light on the distance? Just in front of that, there was the fleet, four boats in total, but how I cannot see them? Explain that for me please, what happen to the fleet?

Worm – As I told you Admiral, that you would not come back with them, you belong to us, and also your family would come likely to reunite with you, and will live here in peace and a lot of happiness all the days that would lived that surely would be a lot, because all of you will die in your old days, I have the shame for tell you that will see great grandsons born and grow up, as you can see, we do not have a menace already anywhere, your ships have been suffocate by our country, we have wont this battle, without shut a single bullet, because we do the war more efficiently than any country. Our governants do not know yet that they won, that they already did their work, and that result from the best form as usual, but it have not said and they do not know.

Admiral – Mr. Worm, please explain to me what was that happening with the fleet, United States will send now a lot bigger arsenal and more powerful, how do they do this, this is an offense, to them do not forgive that you have destroy their four ships, they are people very brave, do not you realize that?

Worm – Admiral, your ships had not disappear, they are there in the bay, only that you and me cannot see them, and if you call them will not be communication, because your love is for us, not with them, is for which your family will come with us, because you already, belong to us, you already fall in love, the United States will not know that their fleet have been neutralized, and that their bullets will not come out of yours canons, because their canon do not have gun powder, better say, they have, but is too old already, they have 150 years in the respective ships, were put there before the material what it was used to build the ship, do not asked me an explananation about that, because I do not know how to explain it that, please.

Admiral – Well, then, now I have to admit without understand that my fleet have disappear, that I live here, that I live in your house, that I am your prisoner, and will be with my family, that I am a deserter, and all that without need of understand what is my life now?

Worm – All that you have say is the true, but not on the way you said, but the same with a sight with a lot more honor, and a lot better motivation. For example, you will not live in out home, but in your own house, you will live in our until yours is finished to build, you are not a deserter, but one who's heart denied to accomplish dishonored and unfair, and an officer of such a high range like you may deny to accomplish such an order like that, an order that do not deserve to be accomplished, and you have not kidnapped, but that is the greatest aspiration of your heart. To live in an environment filled of peace and love for the others, is that you have desired every day, since that you understand the world. We will wait here, before to go to the mountain , until your wife and children arrive, your tripulation will see them arrived, and will live without you, because the tripulation will have no news from you, and will not listen the calls that will be make from the superiors, is not like that who work your channel of command, in front of a superior officer kidnapped?

Admiral – Yes, is like that, but I am not kidnapped, no . . .

Worm – For us you are not, but your government they could consider you are, because they do not know the truth, and for sure will send a committee to investigate all the details that they can, they are determinate to perform the plan that they have the duty of perform. Let's go to the airport Admiral, because your wife and children are about to come, it is going to Shine the son at any moment, and for when we get there the plain should be there already. And your wife and sons will be seated waiting to see you. Will be a happy encounter, for that we will have a good breakfast, prepared there, my mother will take care of that, she knows all the details related with you, because she have taken as he dear son.

Admiral – Tell me sir, please, how is that you are called Worm? Do not result that a little offensive?

Worm – Of course not admiral, that name is due to my father, one of the being really important in the universe, nothing that come from him can result small or offensive, he is the man more noble you can know, never would do to another that may do not receive himself, because he execute the things from the most noble, he never put you smaller at least you enlarge yourself, he put me that name so small, so I can put myself a little bigger with no penalty, but anyway I have tried to present myself small always so he can always be proud of me because I want to be loved and respected by him always, because I want feel be loved by him always. So I make feel to the others which love me, and I feel good with all my loved beans.

All that spoke Worm and the Admiral from the ship of war that send the United States with the purpose of destroy, not only the product that was threatening their pharmaceutical industry, but also to the medical class and also to a worldwide class, but now they have stay without ship and those have disappear with all and the tripulation.

A little time after arrive the plain that bring to the country the children of the Admiral, and his wife, to establish in the country that have being order to destroy, then now it look a like Worm have the situation a little on his side for the moment, we do not know the reaction that will take the

United States before this situation of national defense that have been presented.

Mis. Minerva is coming with her children, low the stairs of the private plain that paid Worm for them, and right away gets embraced and enters in the Worm's truck, and departs for the mountain for the, house of his natural mother where they will stay until their house be dully finished for suit, as we already knows in this country that is moved faster, and surely get finished before the new escolar period, for to the children do not have to make a change of school, which may be important, and in this way are making their plan, the house is located in a piece of land that the president donated for the admiral, a place of 1 ha (1000m2) and the house already had built the base, and the blocks until the roof tall, the windows are already ordered to the manufacturer and so is the central ac and the marmol floor travertine's that are ordered, so the bathroom, and all other accessories to the house of first quality, while the support to build the roof is finish, and it goes beside a teas top over plywood bases.

The news do not stop of been radiating in parts, each hour repeat The same and come back to say it again, had happened so that also talk of the house that is been build for the admiral and his family, news this that alter to the United States, because is the first news that they have over their four ships, nothing are that they could know about of after, because this have come the cause destruction and had been overtaken by the government of the island, they now can be seen and get communication with all, but its flag had been changed by the flag of the island, actual owner o proprietor of them.

Next day, the old proprietor of then, send a fleet of 50 bomber planes with the order to destroy them all the fields where they find green houses and do not live anything standing of those structures, and that bomb the ships and aircraft carriers, plains, and helicopters for assault, contained in the mentioned ships. When the plains bombers arrive the island, a general panic is empowered of all the nation which come out to the streets and the plains see all as green houses, everywhere field and cities, they do not know what to do, 50 planes are not capable of destroy so much space, and so inform to their govern.

At time of the pilots to report such things, they ask them if they became suddenly crazy that suspend de bombing to the frutals, and destroy the ships, but they cannot find them anywhere, a passenger plane, inform that they have seem such ships near Colombia, where are anchorage and enjoy of the beaches accompany from very beautiful women, such are in the water swimming with the marines dressing only with very little tangas, that Luke are not built with clothes, but with dental floss only, but they bearably from 20k feet, and they feel envy, of them because they want to be there with them.

The actual commander of the Us Navy order to the pilots not to shut, because do not desire a open war against the all world, only against the island of Gusmani, who now are the owner of that small float. The president of the United States break into the radio and order directly to the pilots to open fire against those ships with Gusmani Flag, wherever they are.

Before to shoot, the pilot of the fleet, the leader, note that the ships do not have the island flag, but Colombian flag, and under the new consideration, ask for new instruction about how to proceed under this new situation, they are instructed with do not do anything, because that would be a situation of not declared war.

Some minutes after, the ships show up in the bay in front of the capital of the island, in the original formation, that one they never lost, and where they were all the time, and all the tribulation is with them dully uniformed and with the flag of the island, and the pilot ask for instructions, how to proceed before this new situation; the president of the US, got full or courage and anger, order to open fire, to all ships.

Now happen that the ships come and go, on an intermittent way, they do not stay stable, so they can get their position and make fire, they shut random, but they cannot make blank, when they appear is in another gps position, and this mistaken shooting make damages to the marine fauna in the water.

These is all fruit of the collective hypnotization of Worm, have attack to the warriors that are invading his loved island, and there is nothing they can do, but that night, the fleet stay stable in the bay, a perfect blank, no matter the calendar says that is new moon, in the sky there are a full moon, that make a perfect illumination, like it would be a noon sun, then the pilot are ordered to shut, those take off from their airport from the General Andrews airport in Florida, but they are been flying the all day, have been with empty tanks almost, this would be highly risk, and there is no pilot who accomplish with the order of take off, then Worm send chauffeurs to pick up the pilots that had land in the airport of the island, so they come to have a good dinner in the island, mean while the United States send a tank plain to refills the plains. At arrive there, the pilot that is refilling the plains, the pilots did not fit in the buses Worm had send, and were waiting that pick then in a second trip, ant those, invite also to the pilot of the plain/tank to have dinner with them, those who are dying of hunger, because after a all day starving, cannot expect to have anything else, so, happily go with them, the food is served in the restaurant in front to the park, where the fist incident happened, when the visitors attacked a supermarket and a hardware store.

They ate and after Miss Mary who was the leader in charge of that act say to them that: Please all have a seat.

Representative of all the pilots – This is a terrible injustice, and the order given with all that violence, do not deserve to be obey, have being prosecuting to this country, of an unfair way, they have been prosecuting of an unfair way, that who do not have another thing that save them, because are selling to them medicine of good quality at price of refreshing drinks and far from using painful injections, or sour drinks are sweet drinks, and very pleasant also and also that never raise in a rocket the prices, but when that happen will be in a parachute going inverse way. Not as the pharmaceuticals, when an aspirin that cost 100 for less than one cent, they sold for 2 for 50 cents. As they are invited to stay in the island, they say that if the invitation is firm they will accept, and will stay living there.

Miss Mary say, that now she understand why the island had such a low population level and why they did not have massive new born either, probably God had preserve that space for a moment like this.

The United States comment what had happening to England and France, As to Russia, and the three in chorus say that allow then to attack and take charge to see if are your citizens that do not want to accomplish their labor, and they will want to take care of that.

After united States give their consent, the first in arrive are the English, who without advise open fire against the four ship anchored in the bay, statics and fix, they shut high caliber bullets and with bombs heavy weight, but in place of exploit the ships that fall in flames are their proper planes, the bombs are not falling by the gravely, but they take a different lapse, going to where deserve to receive them, not to where they are pointing to. On earth, people are seeing how the people do not walk, they pull their faces out in order to see to the others on a great surprise all the damage that they desire to make are receiving themselves.

The French plains arrive and shut sweet bullets, so, the kids come out to pick up a enormous quantity of those pleasant presents they see fall everywhere, like chocolates, caramels, cookies, ice cream that do not melt quick, and all for kids, they felt extremely happy, those candies do not make any damages and all pass very likely for them.

Two hours later come the Russian planes, which launch bombs against the plains parked at the airport in the island, and that fall is sweet cotton, gofer of corn, more ice cream and soft drinks of every kind without brake, or melt they are all surprises for all this that is happening, all plains direct themselves to Florida for a quick inspection about this situation, because they cannot make any damages against the inhabitants or properties in the country, is all a mission that show contrary to themselves, are imposibilitated of make any damage to who they are considered the enemy.

All the pilots addressed to a building that is used as a church, and that is placed near the airport where land the 1,000 plains, 300 of France, 200 of England and 500 of Russia. At enter and seat in the bench listen a soft voice that talk to them from the roof, and they could listen each one in their own language:

"Do not Occur to attack against my people again, if you do who should prepare to receive you prize will be yourselves, this opportunity will not be repeated, so pay good attention and obey, and go back home."

At listened to this, the pilot ask to the others:

Russian Pilot - Did you listened in Russian what I had listen?

French Pilot – Yes, I heard that, but it was in French, not other language.

English pilot – You are mocking on us, I cleared listened that in English, and I do not speak French or Russian.

Scared, each one claimb to his plain, and after charge fuel, when back to their base.

Surprised, now all the leaders of the countries that have turn against the island decided not to attack again, but to search other means, all came back to its old time, like before the serape, but with good health now. All had returned to the old way, apparently at least, they could see all thing as they always had see them, The United States were observing the island truth their satellites for watching, and say to themselves, that it was that the moment for to launch an attack with regular missiles, and nuclear to finish with all there, so, they started the regressive account for 100 missiles at the same time

Arms and ready to their regressive account were shut with a blank for the plantations of the island, they stay watching by the satellites until that they fall on top of the green houses, and destroy all there, now you will see there, on what was the truth of the happening: They all were watching of the greenhouses but that was what they watch on the previous minute, in that previous minute, in the real minute, what was really in the view was only water, the island had been disappeared and had gone to another dimension in the universe, the rocket fall and all got wet, the normal's and the nuclear causing some radioactive waves causing a tremendous evaporation, that caused a rain for a week, time during which no belie action could be realize , because it was so intense that there was no vision for anything, if extending an arm under the rain, could not see the fingers on the light, in the island that week, nobody went to work, it was a week of vacation 100 per cent, of family dinner were suspended while the rain last.

Those days were the first vacation days in the island since ever. To the president try to use this as the opportunity of mocking of them and call to the president of the United States, then he told to him:

"Mr. president, the people here in the island want to extend to all of you our gratitude for give us the opportunity to have our first ever complete vacation for a complete week, from today, every year, will remember this as the season for vacation due to the American war because this days have been so pleasant and agreeable so, we will continue using then in your name".

p.p. Thanks for the present of planes and ships that you made us, we will keep them due to the need we had and the useful they will be do no send instructors, they have already here and will teach us with pleasure.

The United States have already notice that would not could attack not up front, not by watch, there was nothing that function, there was something in that island that prevent from all the thinking that they could have, what thing could they to do, and to take revenge, and destroy them? "When your enemy is stronger than you, unite to them" that is the formula that surely works why not to used?

Right away prepared a boat of tourist, call the president and ask permission for a group of Americans could go to the island and visit them in a tourist boat with the purpose of make sure of all the goodness of the island, and why their citizens and pilots have choose of to fix their place of residence, instead of keep enjoying all the comfort that they had there, would it that we can do that?

The president of the island answer to the president of the United States, that this country is who invite to anyone in the world, and every one with good intentions and desire of share with us, obeying our norms and uses and who behaves on an acceptable, will be welcome today and any day of tomorrow, as one we did with visitors who wanted to come.

The ship went to the island, in a week it had arrived, in their cabinets there where not common citizens but marines dully uniformed, with their wife's, and their children there were some 5,000 in total, arms of all kinds, Bazookas, automatics gun, 10,000 bullets shells, for caliber 50 and 70,, about 100,000 bullets caliber 40, 10,000 hand grenades, and also launch grenades, guns of laser ray, bombs of dynamite, explosives c-4, in general all that could be hand transported, they wanted attack by treason, and suddenly as always the island has who take care of it, for to be models as habitants has who take care of it.

They all came down from the ship, only persons, they wanted to take an inspection visit, and see the places that they should to attack first, and how should to be done, in any place, went to the beach, they stay in the towns, once all came down, the ship disappear with the arms and all, they have no place where to sleep, they did not have food, so they spend the night in the streets and with hunger, they wanted to assault a supermarket as previous have done, but receipt a discharge electric, that send them 3 meters away of their wall, after this did not try any act of violence, but to return to the harbor of the capitol for to sleep in the ship, and use something of food.

Tremendous surprise they took when found the port completely empty and their ship with 500 feet long, 30 story toll over the water and 3 story under the water, there was not, the presence was limited to water where should be a ship, had disappear, as the other things, that now were visible, because they had change the owner, they ship also had change the owner? What would do the island with a ship of that kind? To the American citizen offered that they can go swimming, because they were not very well received, or that come to pick up, the last offer was accepted, we will send a ship from the marine in which will pick up our people and will return and promise that we will not come back to bother you.

Say the proverb that dog egg eater, no matter they burn the mouth, he will keep been egg eater. Next day appear in front of the bay a ship of war American with some 2000 soldiers, which came down arms of all kind of arms, and walk until ground, but they only saw grass, like a football field, as much they move, same view, nothing new,, and the soldiers who have come to pick them do not arrived, they do not know what to do, the stadium had no end, where already tired, they do not know what to do, were already tired of run and for more they advanced , look back, and the wall was still near, as much they advance they do not advance, it was like they were running over a band of movement, but in the opposite direction, practically at the same speed, and no see another thing but a football field, nothing else, there was not public, of ball, there was not racetrack either, it was exclusively a football field. It was exclusively a football field, after two hours running, come and admiral from the marine and order them to return to the ship, they obey, and when returning to the harbor, the ship is not there either, the tourist ship appear on the opposite side of the island, painted of dark green, when it was entirely white with adorns red and blue, now is uniformly green. The tourist ship sail until the capitol, inside was painted a section of clear blue and another section pink feminine.

The ship of war appear a week later anchorage at a dry propriety of the new Marina of the island, that was equipped with the military presents that the government and allied have been given to them. Now the United States have 7,000 soldiers in the island, that do not have anything to do with the arms and the ammunition left in the tourist ship as in the ship of war, that had been withdrawal and deposited in the arsenal of the army just build because it had been contemplated that peaceful island full of persons of soft character will enter in a conflict of war with another country not necessary to depose the attractants from continue that attitude.

At that time, Gusmani have two month with the war declared, without have to shut not even a bullet to the enemies, and the only missiles shuttled was only to the fishes in the water, and one to the central park this should be of lament, but some 50,000 fishes died with that severe attack beside of those who died for the head of the nuclear bombs that do not appear as a physical evidence all those that were hurts and dead and left a cadaver as evidence, all were counted after than 2 hours after the island was set in place.

In that lapse of time, our friends that have lived for the mountain had arrived and the truly mother of Worm was happy with all that new family that had arrived to visit her, the kids of the admiral were also radiant of happiness and the wife was delight with all those flowers that there was in the front yard of the house, all kind of plays for kids, plays that they could pass 3 days trying one after the other, and do not finished all, playing 5 minutes on each one, the garden of the house had 2 kilometers in one direction, and 10 kilometers in the other direction, space more than enough for that a woman 100% female could see and admirer all kind of flowers that never could imagine that exist, with the odors and fragrances more variety, could get lost if could not get orientate, but could not get lose anybody in the backyard of that lady for more than two hours before she could be found and directed to the right way for that person could go to anyplace that could desire, of returned to the house if it was its desired. Or that it was time to make any one of the foods, there was many kiosk in the house, in case of desire of eat or drink something, this was a 5 star house with all capacity to sweetener the visitors, and as much as the size of the house as the attentions do not have more than the start, it has no end, so everyone arrived at the place where have agreed the admiral will a few days, time during which his residency would be finished and will be able, meanwhile will lived in this palace of rest, a palace with all the commodities could dream, could form her ideal dream, and would not could never, not even close of all that could find never not even close of all that could find here, because there was that and much more.

For the admiral, there was all kind of agricultural, the 10k hetaeras, of the farm would cover all the desires of agriculture or livestock. For ambitious that he can be, and in fact it was. It was planted every kind of agricultural product all kind of animals. It was all covered, it was such an ample variety as nobody could desired, in one word, it has it all, from a simple mustard seed until great fruits and coconut or watermelon.

The night came, and went call all for to have dinner, they all took a shower, the man shaved and women's got their dressing properly, first were invited to enjoy a delicious wine semi sweet done with the all care, thinking in the queen Victory from England, in the last century, but which take the queen mother of Worm, for the lack of a formal queen, the case it that it was delicious, the dinner was served by each individual plate at the style of a formal dinner in the high society, with no detail that fault, the Admiral had never participated in a dinner that way, with 15 pieces for dinner, at finish the dinner they were invited to pass to a saloon at border of the mountain, with a beautiful view of the field in extends, at end of that view, the coral at the ocean cost, the corals, the undulated sea that was looked in two tones, dark blue and white for the waves when hit one against the other it was a paradise view.

About nine o'clock of the night it was all dark, there was a terrazzo that had a white wall at the end, and there was an explained and a zone under roof but with no walls with seats for about 50 people, comfortable seats that if they're not were doing something that keep you busy, you could easily fall asleep, and these kind of seat had that mission, that if you really were very tired, fall asleep deeply quickly.

In the case of someone fall asleep in that place, there was a kind of transport in which the seat of put on top of a mobile transport and this will take you without awake you, to your bed in your room, sometimes very sensitive persons awake, but normal persons get there and stay asleep while transported, this so, because once in the bedroom, the seat get the horizontal position and parallel to the bed, at the same level, then a sheet fall from the ceiling and you keep sleeping quietly.

The admiral, a educated man with all the military discipline of the naval academy of the marine of War North American, could not stay asleep in a terrace, no matter it be so peaceable as that was, his formation keep him from that, if this situation would happen to him, was very brief, and awake promptly, and would go by his own foots, to his bed, because that was his training in the academy, and in his as student was practice continuously many years ago.

So finish that day for the admiral, his wife and his two male children all stayed quickly asleep in that remains of peace and happiness, the peace came from all the environment, the perfume of the garden, the agreeable temperature fruit of the elevation of the land, more than 10 kilometers high, that would produce like 17 degrees of temperature, Celsius (x1,8+32)=Fahrenheit. That temperature invited the persons to use a sheet to be able to rest well, rising this way the temperature like 5 degrees more.

While in the mountain every one fall asleep, at about 9 in the night, in the city there was yet of some uncertain thing and unquiet, more that a normal day of life there. That entire riot that was combat by Worm had been pacified the nation, but the surprise of that entire riot was that it was the first time hat in the island. A place that had characterize for the quiet and peace, never before had been shut a firearm, and that day a cannon bullet from a cannon of 225 millimeters broke a kiosk, the most beautiful of the all country, built by the contractor corporation, property of Worm, built at high cost due to the high quality of the materials and with a fine work of finishing it, good for the garden of a delicate king.

The house of the admiral, had been very advanced, had been installed the roof, the windows were put in place, the marble floor finish lucks beautiful, only need for install the air conditioning, the baths accessories, the ceramics the closets door, the kitchen accessories, the interior doors, the main door, and a few runner doors and windows made of transparent crystal covered of a plastic color bronze, to make harmony with the floor of the house

Chapter 8

At time of awake by the morning, a bell touch sounded at 7 o'clock very early in the morning, after a pleasant night, do not need to be very long to get a remands, and good rest, a complete rest for all the nervous system and muscular, because the day more than all was tense, not a day of much to work, the maintains were placed to some 60 kilometers north of el Pedregal, or the capital, no matter was a way uphill soft during the part of plane surface, more or less, and very uphill during the last part.

After a bath of repair were presented all to the dining room, were was all prepared to waked up, while they change from the bedroom to the dining room was calling to a great voice the smell of the not mosque of the coffee and the smell of the chocolate with vanilla flavor, that had a deep smell that make you speed up to come soon to the origin of that smell. All that delicious smell, awake in your son kind of good sense, and you need to enjoy with that good extraordinary, like a synonymous of a great life, more with the surroundings.

Once in the dining room, to start was serve coffee to the adults and to the children, a delicious chocolate-vanilla, some with oatmeal, and for those who does not like it, plain.

Worm – Admiral, I have excellent news for you, your house should be finished for today, we have 50 men working in it, and the construction is done, and are working now different persons, in all the details of the house, the work of grass of the back yard, and all of the work of finishing on it, you and your wife can go by the furniture and appliances in order to select the furniture's you want inside of the house, to be, Sirs, we are not telling that you need to go, you can be here for a longer time you want, but you will fell more free, and better in your own house, no matter what, and after you may return whenever you want, this is your home too, but you well feel better if you come as visitor, than if you stay here to live permanently. That applies even for me.

Admiral – How long do they last then to build it?

Worm – In general it is a fix period of 3 days, sometimes 4 days, is the normal time, sometimes there are normal period, for example rain, or extreme heat, beside that is from 3 to 4 days, your house was stay as available from when the problem of the 200, nobody in the country own houses, they all belongs to the government, but the houses are assigned to the people the people of the island never had to occupy of that, and as the houses belong to the government, there is not sellers of houses, finally they come out very cheap, the land belong to God, who do not need money, he does not sell the land either, the life here is easy to live/

Worm - Today will enjoy for the first time, a drink of the special serape, for you it will be a king of vaccine preventive as per your health , but is not only medicine, because is also a refreshing drink separate off been a tonic for the stomach acid, this will be very well to the body, you will taste after the breakfast Today, your house is going to be ready, so from this night will be waiting for your decision, to your best convenience, I advise you do not take too much worry on move to your house, the worry was to make it available for you, it will be, so, there is no worry anymore, you move when you find it better and more convenient, yet is still furnished it, you will need to refrigerators, one of them come with 3 liquid dispensers, we installed one in the kitchen, where we put all the necessary to make the food, and another in the dining room where we put the complement of the food, and also the dispensers of the drink, so we do not botter very much, what we do, we do it well.

You will be wondering why the government built and give so many things? Because if do not do that way, then, will have to charge taxes, on this way there is no intermediary, and we can supply them at a cheaper price to the people, we simple play a game a different game, that in the long term result more convenient for all, when someone need to replace one of the things that have in use, call the factory, this send a new one and pick up the old, and rebuild it, after this process, it will not be recognize for anyone, not the users not the manufactory, it looks exactly the same.

Here, every three months we have a meeting to have some food, we burn all the old furniture, those that work no more and cannot be rebuild, so we burn the food and use the heat to cook some food and we have a lot of fun. So everyone take some food from the house and we cook for all, we form a line to have the food, as is a common food and nobody paid for them, there is no complain, at time to eat them.

These public things at what you are not used to, that you do not have any practice over them, at the beginning may result a little uncomfortable because you and your family rather environment more reserved, and intimated, but after a few years, you could not live without them, I assure you that is the simple thing those who bring the most of our life, the luxuries are particularly bored the real happiness is in the puberty but everyone like here, but here everyone have more happiness that in the capitalist system with all that individuality, we do not really are looking for commodities, we look for the happiness, how to be having fun with anything we do happiness with anything and we have discovered that this is done with share, that is why we share dinner every night, so, we do not like to have dinner alone anymore, each family propose what they want for dinner the next night, and what Is not done one night, is pending for the next one, until everyone in pleased, who do not cook, have to wash the dishes, after play something that is available, or watch a movie.

For example, we do not have here great expenses of electricity, we have tree generators thermoelectric, that work one every month, in that way, we have the opportunity for give a o good maintenance to all, and last much more time, that to any other country, we have like 10 times more production of electricity than the expense, the major expense of electricity is the public illumination, and almost all is produced locally, no matter what it cost we do not need very much devise.

The government is actually checking to install a manufacture to make automobiles here that is the only that we are importing, until the tractors agricola are manufactured here, the TV, every house has 7 televisions of 32 and 27 inches and 1 in the spare, these are the only size that are manufactured in the island, because we do not need more, if any get damaged, is taking to the manufactured and it is replaced for another, they are all the same color, form and size, there is no discussion, the manufactory replaced no matter what it has, reconditioned and put it in service again.

There is no need to lie, or deceive, the penalty for lie or intent to deceive is one year without service, you will not have stove, no a/c, refrigerators or furniture, if you have any avery will have to stay without that, that is the penalty for lie or intent of deceive.

Here everything is on good faith, or deceive, for that reason, we hope from all, to act in good faith.

Admiral - Thanks for invite us to live in this paradise, Worm, and I would like to recommend changing that name, for example Gustav, that is more beautiful than a simple Worm.

Worm – That is good, call me that way, the others would like keep calling me as usual, because think that Worm is more useful, work to fertilize the dirt and five us a better grass for the house of for the cattle, or a better food to eat, I do not feel bad, all love me so much as I love to them, and that is what we concern about to me they can call me, shit if they want to, for me that will be a excuse for having a very good laugh. Another motive to be happier. I recommend you much to take the thinks friendly here. Because nobody need to be severely judge here, because we are all looking for a little more happiness, and make happy the others, so, do not take nothing very serious of the necessary, first think in how to be happy yourself, without make to suffer to the others, because that is the north of all and everyone.

Good, let's take breakfast all, otherwise, we will not be happy enough for to support so much fun that we will have in this long day, the thing for the living and all you may need, are in them, there is no need to pay for them, but If you would like to make business, you will have to pay for all, but I do not think so.

Admiral – What happen if someone do not want to work, or cannot work?

Worm – Here we turn every think, nobody are there that do not want to work, all can take some days off, when we want, that is not difficult, always we do not affect to the others, we use to work every day, less the Saturday, so, we all deserve a day of rest, the only think, is that we do not take it when it come to correspond, but when we need it or desire it, now we can take three free day a year, after the Northamerican invasion as a remind of it. We can take one or two days off, that is what is permitted, there is no more than two, we all know that and we respect it, we all take it, and not even have a sickness, we are all very healthy, besides we try to enjoy of everything, inclusive to the work, the happiness is always our north and that we take very serious, never play with somebody happiness, because you will know what you do not need to know.

Admiral – What happened if I am not happy, if always I am taking everything serious, as we do in the navy, for example?

Worm – In the navy you do not take all very serious Admiral, be honest, there are thinks we do not joke with them, of course, not here or there, when something most to be take in serious we do, if you are always very serious, is going to be you the first who would want to fix that, because you will be the first who will lose his happiness , I do not advise that, be more loose, that make us to be always serious is the rigid, is the tension, when you relax yourself it all come fine, and take its place, if you look in our population, in the 1,500 years that the island has in existence, nobody had died of cardiac's problems

The longevity of our population is one of the thinks we are proud of, all our deaths pass of 150 years of age, as you can note, the persons live the double of time than other places that some others, and are 100 time more happy, the worry of self, are for everyone, we do not rest until that had disappear we all live as a single family, we love all one to each other, all love very sincerely, and you would like that, because there is no one here that want to change that, no even an pix from that, what normally happen is that everyone one to be more close to the other, the male love the female, the female love the males, we have to be quick, when you like a girl you have to be quick, and talk to her, otherwise someone else may come and talk to her, and he has her, the first in talk is who has her, when you have one, do not get interest in another, because is where the jealous problem start, for wanted what do not correspond to you, never the opposite. If a girl is available and you talk, you have her, if she made a compromise with another, will tell you that always, here we are honest until dead, you only need to take what you can take, and let go what cannot take, there is no place to divorce here, because the divorce come from the lack of love, and here never there are lack of love, is not due to that, we should not look in the woman or the man of another either, there is not homosexual or lesbian here either.

The homosexuality had never existed here, that is a detour from normal conduct, a mental sickness, for that reason it does not exist, because there is no sickness here. We are all sane due to the serape.

Admiral – Please explained me what is the content in that serape?

Worm – It does not cure anything really, is an psychological effect what it produce, you consider cured and you really are, is an act of faith, only that, the serape is fruit juice with cocaine power, but as you do not take the juice in great quantity, do not get the addiction to it, only you like it and want to keep drinking it, do not have to drink it, same as the water, it get finish with it.

Admiral – When do we go down to town again?

Worm – A little later, if you do not want to stay longer here, do you pas it well here?

Admiral – Of course yes, I would like to live here.

Worm – If you move here, you will not like that much as if you come to visit, because you get use to all, and you start to see everything as normal, the new and the variety is what provide the great satisfaction, and here is not that good to live, as is for coming to visit.

Admiral – I have see the plan, this is one of the largest islands in all the planet, is how what, mid of Oceania, Australia, Greenlandic?

Worm – Is like half of Greenlander more or less, in extension, but here had never had fall ice, or snow, this is an island really very safe, there is no earthquake , or hurricanes, or flood, it is all controlled , there is something that you need to know, this island is protected by a dome, this stop all that comes and is not usual, when the necessary rain fall for the agricultural, or for the generation of electricity the dome set itself, and the extra rain go to the ocean, the dome has the exact form of the island borders, and pick up to the ocean, to access to the ocean we need to jump over the dome always because one food from the water of the dome is always there, it is necessary of pass over it, because it is indestructible. When a ray comes, the dome is put and stops it, the dome last a 1 million of a second to be installed and the same to take off, is practically instantaneously.

We are here very proud of it, it is our maximum protection against the foreign events to us, the same would happen with undesired airplanes or bombs or missiles, we do not receipt those effects and the dome can be put for 100 years without be removed not even for one second, because it evolve the air we breathe it is not just a little of air but all, the dome is not let set, first, because we do not controlled it, cannot put it, or take off, when we like, it only work automatic, there is not a mechanism for that

Worm – Do you want to know the capitol?

Admiral – Of course, yes, it is very near of El Pedregal, isn't?

Worm – Oh, yes, but is near over here, taking a detour here to the left, because it form like a rectangle and the hypotenuse is here, over there should be the rectangle that would take us to El Pedregal.

Admiral - With all the explanation that you are giving me, I could return to my country and betrayed you, have not you realize of that Gustavo?

Worm – Well, I do not see how could you, I have not tell you any news on which we can be vulnerable of on what we really are, tell me something you can do any damage, that you know for my mouth, please, or by the mouth of someone from here?

Admiral – The dome for example, you have tell me about it, now we know, we should to break it and attack later by the hole.

Worm – The dome is indestructible, last forever and there is not a think that can break it, it it make from the same material that is done the atmosphere, never ever fail, and there is no how to penetrate it, is something is that can help you, for example is for protection of the coming flaying object, and do not have permission to land, or to fly our territory, it go to be destroy with the dome, this will put again and the object it will collide with it, not matter what it be, it will get destroy, no matter be a be a bird from the sky.

Admiral - Gustavo or Worm, what would happen, if my wife or children or me, wishes to return to the US?

Worm – Well give you thanks for to consider be one of us and will put to your order in case in the future you want to come back to visit us or to stay.

Admiral – What would happen with the house?

Worm – Somebody else would live in it, maybe myself who knows. Look Admiral, this is already the entrance of the capital, as you can see the palace of government is not in the center, but just here in the outside of the city, and very out, there are 10 kilometers from here to the center of the city, since the president until the most simple people of the government, you can come down we do not need an appointment, the president receive to everybody if do not have something else to do, and ir that is the case, will supply to come back and excuse him for this time, because that should be completely unusual, he normally receive to everybody immediately, what may happen is he be attending to someone else, and in that case will receive both at the same time. The president never make private meetings with anyone, here all can realize all conversations, we can know your things, as you can hear hours the privacy is only for you with your wife to procreate your Childs. All our lives are publics for all, there is no secret, all our lives are publics.

Admiral — And this is the rest of the city capitol, everything else are commerce and living houses. Industries or commerce as anywhere in the country, here we live where you want to all areas are good for living, there is no difference between to live in the capital, or in a town, if you have realize, the population is equally divided more or less the same, every town are same in population, there is no city too big than the others, either there are zones better than others, all zones are equal. There is not buildings like in your country we do not have competences in purpose to see who live in the best place, this is why we play the games at the inverse result, the winner is not really who receive the premium, here, we all want to get the fist but who receive the premium is who get the last. This is the way of appreciation for the other to have the spirit of participate maybe without having the training or the faulted for been a winner. Is a prize to the bravery of the persons to compete in unequal conditions?

You had seen that when you have in your house full of trophy, that do not means you are a winner, but you do not wont and the others gave their prizes for you as a consolation prize, so, that means how good we are here, that we let you to enjoy when you do not deserve anything but you may have consolation and thanks for to compete maybe knowing you will not win, and that is why you have the consolation, but the bravery to do us a favor of participate.

After this, they return to the mountain, and the admiral take his car, pick his wife and children, and go to see their new home, went to the furniture store and return to sleep to the mountain where will sleep that night, before return to the mountain, he went to the vehicle distributor to pick up her new truck and pick up his wife for the first time in their own car which will have in use for several years while living in the island, because from that place nobody will take him out, not even in exile.

On his side, the invaders were not defeated yet, but were keeping doing things to return to the force of invasion, no matter, yet have encounter one way that tells at the point with their interest and yet do not know anything of the dome of automatic protection, their even know how to lift the dome because of the weight, and could not violate for the strong and resistant.

They continue how they did during the beginning of the second war world, some that appear with a solution as appear the commander of a submarine as a strategy as the fillister of David against Goliath, but it pass the time, and nothing happened. Keep going as of the first day.

It come to happen that Germany would be in the country most perjuricaded from all those that were involved, and said that offer for to give a massive attack, but they were in need from the United States for to give them facility the use of some carriers for to be able of start the attack as near of the island as possible, because all were like unstable, and felt unsafe like betrayed that they will see if they could attack by surprise that give them time for to get another dose of collective hypnotism again to them.

United States tell them that all they order and need, the airports carriers are already, also they can send some pilots the airplanes carrier that is very close of the island already, because there was one installed there, with they only have to moved closed to the position where they wanted it. They had move to international waters before, and now had been put it back, it has never withdrew before, so it still available for use immediately, but they had another by 2,000 miles of distance to the island, now had one in the north and another by the south. This last one could be put in territorial waters of the island in less than 24 hours, they can count on that, they offer a caramel if they win.

So, the North American send the carrier to national waters of the island, in an aggressive plan of attack, and the other submarine they put in movement immediately, the German by their side made to take off 500 planes of combat prepared to be hunt and bombers, of mix attack the same were efficient for combat air/air/ or as for to combat air/land, they were planning that with those planes flying almost at land level, will finish with everything in that poor island immediately, in only one run out

At sunshine of next day, the German start the attack without previous notice, or anything they were worst than the Japan in the Second World War, this not gave an advise until that the attacked ignore it until it was late, when they saw the advise, were bombed already, but the German, gave the island anything to ignore either.

The fist advise that the island receive were 200 planes that hit with the dome destroying and getting in fire immediately, they explode as much the plains as the bombs their bring with them they all hit near on top of the capital, but the dome was installed like 10 kilometers up the ground, that is where the atmosphere and this cover, there is not space on top of the island that stay discovered there is protection everywhere.

The German could not understand what happened, because everything was good, could not see anything with the plains could hit anywhere, and do not know any arm that could hit 200 planes at the same time, it was an arm completely new, unknown for gringos and German

The second carrier arrived but before to send anchor disappear. Not even finish to delivery, before than the country could its defense from their attack this carrier with 300 units on top, as previous hunt/bombers, that were equipped for both uses, were very fast, and yet have a capacity for transport some 50 bombs of 500 pounds each better said a cargo capacity of 25,000 pounds.

Now the German are completely lost in an instant 200 plains and all the tripulation they had send some from Europe, as from America, were continue as the beginning, they do not know what to do, immediately they star to pray the

Lord as in Europe, and in hours of the afternoon they got an answer that say:

"The inhabitants of this isle you are attacking, are my dear sons that do not do damaged under any circumstances, and are totally protected by me, Jehovah father of the all world, Creator and future destructor yours, due to your bad behavior, and customs of a mad heart".

They pray all afternoon with a petition but they could not understand the answer, that this were taking, for your bad heart, and worst feelings, the pray used to say that tell them what to do with them, because all that they were doing was coming bad, and this was due to all they were doing was to create damage, and they do not do bad things, only good things for the others inclusive, they had living with them hundred of persons that came from their country, that went to create damage.

Germany and the United States, keep looking a new strategy, and now France and England had united to the attack and decided open fire from some nuclear submarines, in that way, they could attack without seem them, only will live fractions of one second before they can defend themselves, that strategy cannot fail, so they send 200 submarines entre Germany, France, Russia that united to them at latest time and the United States, the submarines bringing normal bombs as well as nuclear, ready to be fired.

The submarines surrounded the isle, and they put them everywhere and start shutting they arms immediately but this time the dome did not work properly, and the arms did not hit in their blank, and they hit to the submarine on the other side of the island, the bullets did not follow the original trace, but they follow their own, the computer got crazy and shoot to her own friend, something that could call friendly fire, from a friend to a friend. Before so much friendship from people little friends could not expect a better treat, and it happened the third plan.

The Chinese and japans put themselves to make a tunnel that go across the planet thru the center of the planet and hit them by below where it couldn't be a dome. While making the tunnel, the heat was consuming the workers a few kilometers to get to the center of the planet, the machines that were transporting the machine that was performing the earth, with the heat of the center of the planet died asphyxiated the operator of them.

In four attach received from the 7 richest countries more powerful of the world, the island have not receive any damaged yet, because are protected by the only being from which you need protection, Jehovah God, Creator of the universe and destroyer of the same, all at the same time, at least for this 3 err time, we already know about two of them, plus this 3er time, and if there will be more, we do not know yet.

This is the most peaceful place in the world, not even because they have attack several times, looking for our annihilation, with no mercy or compassion, have been attack with the purpose of destroy them absolutely at all, only because they had offered the good of the medicine, they were offended at the point of desire their dead and disappearance, did not satisfy with enjoy the good they are doing, but desire the bad by complete for who do the good, in that way, forgetting the bad that Nebuchadnezzar received and beyond the happening to his son Balthazar.

That very same night the admiral listened the news about the attack Americus/German, as well the attack Chinese/Japan, surprised for so much aggression, launch some figures of cartoon, that are written this way: symbol of #, sing @ & $! # And other symbols that people of bad character knows much better than me.

Admiral – Good that I came here, with the victims, where we can see are the strong, the really powerful, and by invitation and insistency of them, I fell really, privileged and proud of have been accepted.

The dog of bad habit still been with the bad habit, not matter you burn to him the mouth, will keep the bad habit. With all that had happened to the invaders, and do not surrender or admit the disaster or the defied, from which are been object, now are preparing for to make another invasion. Prepare a plain, that will live from Mexico City with some 300 people in total but really will go some 350 people in an Airbus 300 that will live from Mexico, to land in the capitol of the island, in a tourist visit, because the people have curiosity for information of the things that are happening over there, Also will live another from Costa Rica, and another from Caracas, with the same finality and the same arrival date. That is the official news, the truth is that in every plain are going 300 soldiers of the well trained Navy Seals, and the real plan is that carry is it could be very different from that, the real truth may be very different.

The plains live from its original place every one, and star arriving in its time each one at a different hour, but they are coming as the same group, are coming 50 people that speak Spanish, women and children among them and the 300 marines very well armed, but are bringing their arms under their clothes, that apparent to be civil, on their way to walk and the way they wear.

The one coming from Mexico land and the passengers are transported to the beaches of the north region, are coming there by night time, get installed all innocents, the passengers as well as the hosts, all acting with their pretended good faith, but with the truth hidden.

Like two more hours later land the one coming from Costa Rica, with a population similar and the same constitution, arrive to his destination, and act like the first, the authorities from the island, receipt to all as tourists, and take them to the beaches that are at the west of the capitol, to the end of the island.

At fall the night arrive the one coming from Caracas, and those are take to the hotel in the east of the island, were are the most comfortable for children, where you can walk a long way, with the water is still low.

The tree plains had arrive and 900 men armed until the tongues, and to nobody in the island had occurred that this could be a treat of the gringos but those dogs eat eggs no matter you burn the mouth, do not change they will remained the same way. Among those soldiers came many that speak Spanish, so they have no much communications problem. Because it was necessary that was like that, because other thing had been suspicious, and had been discovered quickly, on this way they will need to identify themselves to change the treat to them, and how they are located in different places, with long distance among them, they had to select a meeting point and all the movement had to be by ground, the nearest are at about some 600 kilometers of distance, that means some 12 hours of way, with some who knows very well the area, for to go driving, from east to west are 800 kilometers, about 16 hours for someone who knows the way, because every time they enter a town, need to take another three or four times to make turns in order to take the toad that continue the route. Not all the, town the road keep straight, because with the grown of the town it was necessary to make those changes, like 50 years ago, it was straight, but no any longer.

Worm – The case is that now, they entered the island, and are ready to attack, the news will be a surprise for all, now there is no dome, are in, now can make many things, they are 900 armed men against a population of only 10 million people disperse all along, what is that they can do to defend from this?

Admiral – What thing we will do to defend the island? Need still like 6 hours to reunite, but the arms have the most the group of the east, not other group have arms at importance, but pistols of 15 shots and some additional charge of ammunitions.

The admiral keep a radio transmitter in his truck from the ship when the fist invasion, and is listening a conversation among the group of the north, and the group of the west, those are coordinating to get together all three groups near the capitol, kidnapped the president and take the country, and get that the United States want, that is the strategy. The admiral stay shut, and do not comment anything, let the radio to talk but he do not say anything, so, his wife listen, but do not suspect anything either the child.

Call Worm by the cellular phone while low the volume of the radio to cero, and say, There is something that I do not understand of the house, I am taking the family to your mother house, I will calling you again when coming down, to see if we can reunite and talk about this and maybe some other thinks also, turn on the radio at a high volume, take his family to a safer place, and come back to the capital, meanwhile is coming considering how to make a plan to cut the way to those men.

Once he left the family at the mountain, and say that he will come to sleep with them, that he need to look something urgent, that should not pass over night, so, he need to clear it that day, he will explain to her at his return, meanwhile, trust me.

In his return, call Worm and tell him immediately:

Admiral – They have people infiltrated already in the country, it was those which came in the three planes, it was a trick they used and now the island is invaded, and we need to plan some strategy to see how to combat. I am a militar trained, in order to disarm and to know the terrain is the best strategy in this moment.

Worm – Let them come up to El Pedregal, I will come out of town, let's get together at half way there is a gas station, the only one on the way is by Km 64, the fist that get there, wait for the other and let to know that had arrived.

Worm is relaxed, because he has a no fail plan, but the admiral is felt some unquiet because of the situation, only his military training let to keep in control, is going driving at 90 miles an hour, go like a ray, is only on klm 98 and need to get to 64. Worm know that number by memory, because is the gas station where he stop to get the gas, when in route to the mountain, to her mother's house, and he always buy there to take to her every time he go to visit her, over there always he buy son figs that she love to much, she love them, but never get them, Worm always buy them for her, so, as she like them so much, any quantities she may have in the house is going to eat them, so she let that for him, and on that way is not very fat, she does not need to remind to him, that is like a permanent commission for him, whenever she knows he is going to her, she imagine eating them already.

On the other hand, his hosts go up, softly to 40 kph, letting the admiral, to arrive first anyway, is going to be him who drive in the return, because the admiral need to go as a passenger because is him who know better the zone, where he will take to get together with the invaders. While his get information of their position over the radio.

The admiral get to the meeting point, search for Worm and do not see anywhere, do not see Roberto's Truck either, because of the pressure forget to call him, so he took the cellular phone and call him immediately.

Admiral – Where are you coming Worm?

Worm – By kilometer 50, be patient, there are time for everything

The admiral, warn Worm, that is a very dangerous people, they are very well trained those man are capable of many things. In normal conditions, only one man can take charge of 100 others enemies, but Worm tell him not to worry, they are not to have opportunity to pull their arms for them, you will see how is the divine defense.

Worm arrives to the meeting point, call the admiral,

Worm – Come to over here, please,

Admiral – All of them work for mi at some time directly for me and I know those are well trained men, I listened over the radio and recognize the voice of some of them, also listened the names of some, so I am completely sure of who are them, first we are going to meet 300 of them, later will come other 300 coming from the west, and will get together at the capital, so those coming from the north will reunite with the other with 300 also near the capital, they are transporting in stolen trucks, so, they are going to have no consideration at all, only they will have consideration to the soldiers.

Worm – You are telling me that do not be afraid, haven't you listen what happen to your own ship? Is that you already forgot that scenery or what happened with the planes? We are not alone in this island, we may not have an arsenal to drain blood, but have another kind of defense, that do not to have an arsenal as you know, our arm are of another kind, not military there are a different way that also keep in better shape the health, have not you realize that we cure anything in the people with narcotic drugs? What is rare, if we fight the enemy with only the thinking? From now you are my witness admiral, this truck will not receive not even one shut, nothing will touch us, and we are going to confront with 300 people experts, fine, now you will see how we fight directly to them this day.

Admiral – Is there a bathroom around here, need to go urgently, by the way would be one by those surroundings?

Worm – I am going to stop around here, this is the most similar to a bathroom that we will find around here, but as this is an emergency...

Admiral – It is all right, only need to make pis, because I drank too much serape while waiting for you at the gas station, that is all, do not you think I am scared, you have pacify me, because I with due arms confront alone against an army of them, I had the opportunity of trained some of them when I was a colonel, like 3 years ago.

Before get to the town, turn in the direction of the capitol, in order of surprise the first 300, before they get together with the other 300 coming from the west because if they stole trucks they most come by the main road, there is not accessories roads, this is all straight. As do not present many disasters there is nothing to worry about.

They pass the capitol and keep going to the East, they are not passing because they ask to a transient and tall that they haven't.

Transient – I have liked an hour walking and have not seen any one like that, but I have your number, if I see something like that, I call you immediately.

A few minutes later see some 6 trucks coming and bring many people each, in the rear, of everyone, can see them because they are on foot, and yet the sun is shining, because is still up, it had been a beautiful day, and the light is still very enlighten, the vehicle can be seen clearly, no matter there are not much traffic by the highway.

Worm stop the truck at the right, go across the highway, and make a stop sign to the convoy, this obey and stop all to the right side of the highway, Worm go to the driver of the first truck, who drive to the chief and say:

Worm – Who are you, please and where you go in this moment?

Captain of Invaders – You do not need to know that, better tell me who are you? And why you stop us, to that friend of you I know him, and already imagine who you are, Make then prisoners right now.

There were some 40 men in the rear of the truck, who got down looking to accomplish with the order of his commander, a soldier with the rank of colonel. Those after coming down, and point their Assault's rifles of 30 shots and some with 70 shots. The admiral sees them revise that action and suddenly think in take suicide measures before so many men and worm put his arm in the front while tell him, let this to me admiral, please. Suddenly make a movement with his mouth and the rifle twist like plastic flexible that has overheated the engine of all the trucks start to smoke like overheated , the colonel and the driver that are going on the front get scared greatly , pull out their pistols, with his hands trembling, pull the trigger to shoot to both, but that came out is soft candy that worm pass his finger softly by the point of the cannon of the gun and take to his mouth, and invite the admiral a little in order he to try, and order to the group

Admiral – Get down from the trucks all of you, and walk in front until the capital, where you will be arrested as prisoner of war.

They took those 300 men to the capitol, to a plaza, and release them there, later they scalped and went to the airport looking to return to the country where they came from, look around for the three airplanes they used to come, but they are not where there, only could see three donkeys in place eating from the grass that was very green, as there was not much traffic the grass was growing up faster than another places, and those donkeys were very happy eating that green grass with an exquisite smell to green that was eaten with pleasure, and they found it to their entire like.

At not encounter the plains there, they return to the park of the capital where they were put before, but the truck were not there either, they were abandon at their entire luck, apparently, but not really, a little late, arrive some women like 20 of them in a scholar buss taking food for them and of the serape, that would means a expended food, later, they take their coffee, and hot chocolate, no matter that it was the month of September, there was not heat, but was feel a soft air and fresh in the shade.

For one side, Worm and the admiral, were going from the west, mean those men from the north yet has no time of get to the capitol but were on the way and were like 20 kilometers to get from the airport, on the other side, the radio was offering the news to the town, of were arrested 300 soldiers, and were another many more men but the admiral, and Worm were for them and those do not fail, so, they will detain they for sure and will extract to the people from their tremor.

They had the same strategy as the first 300, they were coming in stolen trucks and at high speed, but suddenly, they found on the way a very big and deep hole on the way, where all the trucks fits there, there was also a wall before the hole that the trucks trough out made out of concrete, at Worm arrive there, pass over the hole in his truck, and over the trucks and over the soldiers and get together with their captain of the soldiers.

Worm – All of you are under arrest, for the government of his country, do not make opposition.

No matter the hole had disappear from their sight so like the wall of contention, the highway was free of obstacles while the trucks do not move, they try to ignore his order, they put the fist gear accelerate and the truck do not move still, got down the driver and the leader, and fall like mangos to the highway, could not expect this to happen, the truck was lifted for over one food from the floor level, so, they hit themselves to remove the powder of the road from the uniforms and ask again.

Soldier – What should we do, were you taking us?

They tell them that follow them, and to do not try to detour to anywhere, because that will be unsuccessful, at arrive at the central park in the capital, were there waiting for us the women with coffee and hot chocolate that they broad extra for the previous prisoners, so as food of the same kind for they to be fine.

They already had 600 of the 900 men who try to invade the island, those that the enemy had send secretly and with their respect, and with all that and respect they had jailed and lose in the park in which have converted in a jail at Alcatraz stile, a jail with no perimetral walls where the prisoners could escape but there was not were to go, with ships or planes, there was no escape, could not go far, this was a jail where they were likely, because this was a jail with the all comfort you could like, can make sports, exercise yourself, walk as long as you can, good food, coffee, all the things that do good to the body and the neighbors used there.

They found the last 300 coming from the west like to a 100 kilometers west of the capitol, but these in place of bringing to the capital, were take to the hill, to Worm's mom house, the gentile lady that was giving lodge to the family of the admiral. At get there, she was very happy, at sight of her dear son, and told him right away:

Lady Rupert —What are those trucks out there? Explain me please; are those from the radio, those that were in lack?

Worm — That's right, the group is now complete, I am needed with advise of what to do with them, how to proceed with them, if we return to sender or we keep them.

Miss Rupert — Invite them to stay, if they want to, otherwise that go as they came in their own donkeys we do not need them we have always only one, and it has been enough, do not bring any more, talk to them, but if they stay, this be for their own will, not as prisoners.

Worm — Get down of the trucks, to all of you, and form lines to ask you a question to all, after the soldiers form lines he ask to them: What do you really want, return to your country, or you like to stay to live here?

The captain of the group told them that they need to return to their country, but that he want to comeback, because the group did not want to live the water at the beaches, they were very likely over there, they spend the all night in the water, all can be see very clear it do not show like night at the water, it was very illuminated like a late afternoon with no sun at all, a kind of penumbra.

One of the soldiers that had the rank of sergeant raises the voice and said.

Sergeant – That should be for you captain, but in the particular I want to stay here, in this paradise, what I need is to bring my wife over here, to live happy with her here in the paradise of God, where the guns cannot be firedog, several times try to shut my rifle of assault automatic, and this never shut, inspect it and everything was fine, same happen to another group, when he try to attack to this man and to the Admiral of the navy, the assault rifle did not work, but to took out candy by the cannon, but this is to give to my wife and kids, that she give me a good life, better of that I could give when was a civilian o what I could give them otherwise, this was the only resource I had. And several said.

Chorus of soldiers – Of course, we also want to stay since now, I am alone and would like to know the local girls.

The employees of the farm opened a great tent for 1000 persons and then all went and got protected for this, they offered coffee and chocolate, serape and general foods for all, in excellent quality, as for guess of a 5 star hotel the tent was decorated inside with night table for each one, and in place of beds on the floor, were put cabins for 2 beds, but for the officers were offered single beds.

That first night had pass, in the morning, after breakfast, the admiral said to the group:

Admiral – Sirs. Let's do something, those who wish to stay do not do anything, and those who wish return to the United States, come out of the tent and put under the shade out there, to solve this matter.

Mrs. Rupert – One by one, please come over here please, for my tailors take yours measures to make clothes for all of you, I am talking about civil clothes, do not worry, we have a tremendous plantation of cotton and we have a large production of would because we produce a large amount of sheep, so we can make as much clothes as we want, any way there is no cold In here, but with that combination, we make a cloth that is very comfortable, and also very resistant, besides we have a divine system of calefaction, another thing is, do not believe that you are arrived to heaven, no matter we are close to that, the people here died and also get old.

They made a line and the Taylor and his helpers took their sizes for all, (the 900 persons in total) and among the 21 people took the sizes of all those persons, they also show the kind of clothes that they will make the clothes, they made clothes for the daily life, for work and also elegant clothes for the especial events, particularly, the event religious, marriages, all occasions in general, also they invite them to make a ride for the all the country, so everyone took note all of the details of every zone, and could make a selection of the areas where they want to live in order to build their houses, with the characteristics they use to do there, because everybody use to live in the same kind of house, did existed in the island a team of people that could build like 500 houses at the same time, in less than 1 week, every time there was a couple that get married a house were build, for when they returned from their honey moon, already have their own house, as it should be.

The soldier came out in buses, and stop in every town that were in their way, so as for every zone in the country where people used to live, the soldiers were coming down from the buses, at time to find the couple they like and want to share the rest of their lives, fall in love, maybe not so beautiful as the model gringas to the like of Food , they swear eternal love, that never will separated and will be together forever, also was shown to then the places for recreation, beaches, the lake, and the place in the beach for lovers.

All worker to the six months of work had a few days of vacation, depending how many days of rest have take, and one of the soldiers said, Oh, with so many days free, the people do not work here, and the mother of Worm said loud:

Rupert – Here, certainly, we do not live for work, but we work to live, and what more pleasure cause to us is to make the think that give us pleasure to make, you will see that in the vacation days we also work, because when someone need us, for a labor call us, and we go to assist with no doubt because help our friend is something that give us pleasure, you also will find that we work day and night and holidays, work never stop, that is why, when someone need us, we assist, because when we call them we want them to come. So, we always please the others.

At time to finish the round in the bus, these were completely deserted, everyone had stay in some place he did like, and were in company of the girls they like, and will be their wife's for the entire life and all will live happy forever, assist to the religious events, the sports events and the community.

Chapter 9

By it side, the enemies do not stop in their purpose, still continue talking with their partners to plan new strategies of how to attack to the island again, but nothing new that would be productive come to happen because all their ideas result that the defense of the island had then covert resulting a expense fruitless.

But they never resign to an island of 1000 kilometers squared win them in the war, they were looking as they used to, that they surrender to them and Neil in front of them, praying for a pardon and to let them to live asking forgiveness for the damaged that they could cause to them, for the damage to their industries and the medical class, which is superior to all other profession in the world, for been the one that support the live on going. But they could not understand the truth, that the fire arms are not the most important arms, either the most powerful, that love and comprehension are more important that another recourse existent in the world, and forever a winner, that will be like in a dream, that always win, and nobody can defeated.

Now the island has some thousands of new inhabitants. The island that had been delayed from its natural growing like the other countries suddenly getting even to the rest of the world, at least for the number of its inhabitants per squared kilometers, in this had increase, but had not get better in their faith, in this they should increase much yet, they were not expecting they have the faith in high as Worm, but better on what by the day they came.

Came one of those days big in the island, and felt overfly plains of war over the island, no less than 1000 f15 and also f17 flying at low flight, and also some bombers flying a very high level, and on what all were seeing is that the dome, were allowing them to do this, and they were asking, is how could them do that, the protection against invaders were not working, and this was due to they knew they have a festivity, and were simple triyng to make pressure with their presence, they had no plan to make any shooting that they, and since there is no danger, they need no protection, they only were taking pictures, everyone were wearing their best and more elegant clothes in order to assist and look fine in the presence of the Lord. The reason for which the dome was not put, is that it notes that those planes were discharge completely, so the Lord allowed them to overfly the territory of the island, inclusive they were allowed to land, and take off if they would want.

We now already who installed the dome, who was who handled the fire arms, and the all system of protection for the island. In hat great gala, all the young foreign were accompany of pretty young lovely girls, some of which have already got married and another's were still groomed and bride but had a happy look, one of them got sick of care, because cannot take the serape of Worm for another complication of health he had, and that afternoon went to visit him Miss Mary, the mother of Robert and Worm, and this last accompany her in that visit, she told to the young man whose name was John:

John – I have tried, and that was caused a tremendous stomach ache.

Miss Mary – Ok understand and follow the advice of this old woman. Do not make pis for 3 days, and, please, do this at least to please this old mother, who wishes with all her heart to see you healthy and running as you use to, because this sickness had prevent you from use your new suit, that my sister had order for you. And will make you to look finally elegant, those suits are not only elegant, but there are specials, very comfortable, you will fill like been in a system of acclimatization, that keep the temperature of your body under 26 Celsius, normally is between 22 and 24 degrees Celsius, a very pleasure temperature, besides that, are soft like silk, no matter are made of cotton and wool, but a wool very soft that do not hurt ever, but will make, that no matter the temperature get low you do not feel cold at anytime. At the time Miss Mary say those words, John was taking a big glass of serape entire of Strawberry and start to make a good sense in his body as medicine.

A few minutes later the young man could not stay in bed,

John — Excuse me, to remove my pajamas, and put the pants of my elegant new suit, because also want to know, if you can take me until the nearest church, because, for sure that some of the assistant will bring me back.

Robert interrupts to say that:

Roberto — It is not necessary, because the nearest church is only at make a left turn here, and ad the next block to the right, is going to be less than 100 meters, you can walk that, but as you ask to take you there, we will take you in my truck, that you have never ride in, is the most beautiful, because my mother was who choose it, when I was 16 years of age, now I already have 18 years of age.

John — Miss Mary, do me a favor, tell me, is used of this island, to invite to ask to everyone who come to cause damage in this island to asked them to stay to live here, because to all of us you gave lodge, to the admiral also, to the Mr. English who live in the mountains, are many bad persons, how you treat all of us so well, when we came to cause you damage?

Miss Mary – Because none of you had the intention of cause us damage really, but had orders to cause damage to us, it was no really something born inside of yourselves, but in another's but of others, you are really sane persons, that other were try, of contaminate, if you return to live there, you will no longer like to continue with that work, but will have to restart again since cero, that is why you now live here with us, in the society you always desire to be, same as the Admiral, and the English Rupert, they had discover the good that is good.

John – Robert and Miss Mary arrived to the place where was celebrating a wedding for 10 couples, what never in history had happen in the island, but is that those young man were so happy with their couples, that they did not want to be alone anymore, but to be completely together, decided to procreate children's, and in that order they must to be married, the girls do not accept that before to get married, it was their used and they do not desire to change that.

Now that the young were getting married, are local girls the band do not desire to go back, because they will be more happy for ever, is that they practically have getting crazy, in that remains of peace, is possible to say that in any other part of the world, because the peace and the justice are that who put the north to all aspects in life, and is so how you may live under the cover of the all Mighty God,

But the bad do not let of being so, look like are like that forever, but it be for real? Let's see now, what are going to do, are making a plan of rescue, their man are like prisoners of war, and for that reason, they believe they are in their right to rescue them, and returned to the bad life, to their train of madness, to their desire for revenge, for to believe that their people are passing it bad, because at this high do not understand that they are having this good life, a life more delicious that never had have until now, and that forever will, because really it does not exist.

But for the arrogance gringo, will always be in front in all happenings in those they are into, because the defeat they had with the war of Vietnam, their roll of make as international police, but not the Interpol, was in interdiction, now with this little island do not come out with, especially, that yours is not really yours. but ours that we are the country of God, that do not believe in him, but we are of the only God, now pretend a pacific invasion, an invasion at stile antique, a mission of rescue, reunite to volunteers, from all religious sects that operate in the country for they to join to recover friendly to its compatriots, prepare a ship of passenger again, call over the phone and say that they want go to an religious interchange, and a mission from the country, a national mission will go to their country in representation of all religious that operate in the country, that please do receive them.

The ship gets prepared, with 1500 passengers with the objective of recover the military and civilians that did stay living there, a large quantity of people from the same country, the ship get to the harbor in the capital and several persons, real personality of the religious world of today's world, those persons we see every day on TV, sometimes in different channels at same time, because, sometimes the same program is passed in different places at the same time, some times, various of them go together to the same presentation, some curious and other invited as paid representatives.

Chapter 10

At time of arrival, worm go to the port to receive them, in the company of Miss Mary and Robert, who get into the ship in the main saloon dining, where fit all the travelers plus the visitors, give then as welcome, ask them to get down of the ship and come, to perform their meetings. Conversations, oratories to the Lord, and all of their interest, that came to do with the nationals, the convivial with the people, go to know the form of life of the people how to live the population, how to live a person in good faith, under the shade of the Lord, go and enter house after house, first to the house of the more rich, then to the representatives of the president of the country, and also how live the more poor, the persons who dedicated to clear the backyards, of the all the houses, how live the farmers, that work in the country, visit the zoo, where the national predators, and foreign predators. The time came for to make a pray and the word have Robert that is who have the best verb of the group.

After finish the pray, are invited again to get down, and come to the place of pray, largest, while they bring several scholar buses, and are invited to get down and shared with the citizens as they know the purpose of their trip, they do not want to stop them, on that way, they can do, whatever they want to, they can do their work, speak to the people, with their people, those they send to commit suicide, but they are protected and gives support including those that were sick, now restored.

Enter in the largest place, with capacity for more of 5,000 people sat in individual seats, and there they meet with citizens of all kind, but at this time that feel incapacity of identify to their compatriots, who did recognize many of them immediately, but as they do not have any intention of return, do not have intention of return with them, do not have any desire of been recognized. At next day, by the radio of the news in the island is heard a communicated saying that the ship came to pick up any one who want to return to his country, are welcome, to present themselves to the harbor in any moment to be recovered and duly repatriated. A commission of them is addressed to the government palace during the second day, to deliver a letter send by the president of the United States.

Such commission was received immediately by the president, as he used to, receipt also the letter from they were ambassador, and was read in public such letter in the presence of the president of the isle, who wanted to reply immediately the same way, in public. And did it in the same terms:

President of the isle – Be you very welcome to this our isle, where all lived as brothers, had not done any exception at receive you promptly but, that this is the way we receipt to all our citizens, the president of the isle do not have escorts, or live on an exceptional, besides any ordinary citizen, we do not make costly elections to change a president, but we promote a tern of candidates and the people make their choice in a written decision next day, in that way the people elect his mandatory, any way who is choose as president will do his role in the most efficient possible.

You have listen over the radio news, have bring the greatest news that we could listen, because here we are in peace, that there is not news what to give, so, repeated all the time that you have come with the purpose of made another pacific invasion, now with the purpose of rescue to your citizens, thing that we are not opposed at all, by the contrary, our mayor like is that the people live as the best possible way, so we will never will impose our system to them or any other person at all, no matter we are convinced that there are no better way to live than ours, that is way, we have tell to everybody to go to your ship and talk to you, and anyone who want to go, that go with you, no matter, we are convinced they will not find a better way of life than the one now are enjoying, or will wise to return, they will choose to stay. And they are welcome to do so.

Tomorrow will radio transit that you are inviting them to a food with you in the ship, I do not know if you have food for so many, but it will be supply free for you also if you ask for it at your request only, but what we are looking is that you have the opportunity of known their life style I warn you, they are going to ask you the same invitation, because our government has behind of the normal poblacional level very low as a country, our density in population is very reduced so out capacity to produce or provisions as food, is very superior to any other country who had deficit in produce food, can contact us and with much affection will sell to them in the quantity that they may need.

Out There was something that had Worm always has disturb, and was all the out environment in torn to his origin, about his bird, nothing about that was clear ever for him, and for him have arrived already the time to get to knows the truth in torn to that mystery of his bird, which was the reason of all of those things he did or say, it finished happening like that, like if God himself were doing, because it come happening as hi say, why suddenly hi had turn to be command in that country, how suddenly, he had doing so well selling fire arms to the weak , and the enemies of them never prosecute.

But what he want to understand was that happening with the serape, that was not that fruit juice with cocaine diluted in it, and how suddenly, this had come to be a medicine kind of panacea that help in everything, Did not understand nothing of everything, for him all had been so weird, always had accept all always, on very good reason, but all that was in need of putted in clear, this was so weird, that already was a need, and who was in place for that were his mother, his real mother, and needed to go back to the mountain, to receive light in that dark night, but clearly positive.

With all ideas in the head go in his truck for the mountain, with the head a little disturb, after put all that ideas, he felt a little confuse, now all look for him like something unexplained.

Now with those late ideas in mind, it was suspicious but a suspect was not enough? So, he will continue until give light to all of this.

At to get there, he star to call her loud, like a desperate, he was not himself, the man as always, he was acting like a child very young, he was not himself, he was crying all the time loud, that he was heard in all the mountain, none employee who has his mother that not hear him cringe, this could be heard elsewhere, they could be hear low in the hill and until the entrance of the caves, it was a farm large, but was a powerful voice, sounding from the top of the hill, and the mother sow up suddenly and worried, no matter she had suspect and expecting that someday, maybe in the moment that less expect, he will show up with all those Doubts for that reasons she had reunited all the proof that her husband have given to her from who was and what he was not, and that his son would come to be, for all that he had made a document signed by him.

At seeing her mother, ask him for what was that had him so excited, what reason could have him so excited, what thing could be happening, because he always had been a calmed boy, and do not used to all these uncontrolled moments, for that, it was for her that correspond find out the reason, and calm him, for that is that she is coming to him without to think, without doubt, without to lose a moment, she present immediately.

Rupert – Here I am my son, let's see, what that happening to you. What had turn you crazy? Come, tell me and resolve together what is bothering you, if I do not have the answers, we get them together but I need that you calm your spirit, and find the peace necessary, I never had denied anything, and will never do, either never lied to you, and never will, will not started today, I always had speak with the truth, understand, comprehend me, and tell me yours doubt, what is that cause this revolt in you.

Worm – Mama, it's that I do not reach to understand all that I do, I am not an individual like the others, I do think that nobody can do, all those think I do for example, the serape, the people that I cure, the wonders I do, the fire arms I convert in plastic, generate heat, the plumb bullets I convert them in plastic, generate heat, the bullets I change for candy, can not understand the reasons, the other people, do not understand not even a part of that, talk to me also of my father, I do not know absolutely nothing abo him, want you to be so gentile of give me reasons?

Rupert – That is for what you do not understand what is happening with you, because you do not know about your father. He was a been very special, he was not a normal human bean, like you or me, he came in a space ship and build another here, the one he departed in, come and I take you to it, there are all the rest of your answers you need, in order to think and comprehend to yourself, and what you do, your decisions, but they are thinks that brought inside of you. And you perform, because you are conditioned for to be good and for do the good, your father did not want to have more sons for the high risk of to get contaminated with the world that is not good, this is a bad world, and the people that live in it also.

Come over here, come, do you see that high point there> that is the space ship that your father land there, got damaged and could not use it for to return to the stars, but in the time that he lived here, that was like 200 years, repaired even build another the one that he used to go, that was like build the arc of Noah, he last a great time to build it and return to his place of living, because he wanted to that you have his old toy, and build another bettered . My son, you do not know how fortuned you are at having a father like that. I am telling some of many explanations. But will live you alone and you will take the time to see and understand all the things that are not giving you the necessary peace, now I feel better, because I see you calm, and is like that how you need to be for to be able to understand all the things that are presenting to you, look remove a little of those brush there, with this knife I have brought.

Now press that blue bottom, so the door opens.

Worm – I doesn't open mother, do not open, how do we do now?

Miss Rupert – You are the son of your father, sure that you will find your answers needed, I am a woman and cannot understand those details, that God created apparently for that only the men could understand and work with them. Now you will have to analyze and search for the answers to can open the door, maybe with the years it have been here, the electric generators had been turn off, and do not start. Half of the electricity of the all country is generated here from this ship, and the other half from hydroelectric, the thermoelectric generators you see elsewhere, are empty, do not have anything inside they are to despised the enemy who attack us, the generation of electricity is one of the points where the enemy attack to make you weak.

Worm – For that is that have been fault of electricity, the streets had been in the dark lately in son places, in front of the warehouse from we dispatch the serape to elsewhere there is not electricity for more than a week and nobody can tell me why. Now I search for the electric man of the manufactory so, he see this and fix it.

My son, do not do that, this machine is a secret nobody knows, is for you to fix it, I know you will be able to do that, will leave you alone now, do not search for help now, nobody should help you, is for you to fix that when you understand the circuits, now will live you, the answers are in there open it and will find your answers.

Worm started to find out, and look for everywhere, the ship was circular, it had like 10 meters high and a circumference of 100 meters, it was a big thing for our world, in a space like that would fit like 500 people sat, what we had to look is if she would be able to lift that weight. He was searching and thought that the fount of power of the ship should have to be in the outside, but where? There are many compartments all sealed, the material of manufacture of the ship look like titanium, is a color like old gold but is more dark, , inclusive of old gold, is almost iron color when is clean with no rust, or much carbon, is a weir material, her mother returned and said:

Miss Rupert – Your father choose this island, because she contain great mines of titanium, that the element he needed to build the new ship, and is the material he was needed in order to fix this, it broke a door when entered the atmosphere of this planet, and was losing its capacity to hold the breathing air adequately.

Now Worm has some answers that alone he could not find, he turn to go, as soon as Worm understood, he calls her again, and asks her:

Worm – Do you know where is the door to get to the fount of energy on this ship, because I need to know that, otherwise would have to open a great number of hatches and doors, maybe difficult to open, and her mother said?

Rupert – I do not know where that found may be, but it would be behind a door, because your father always entered to repair the ship standing up, now have less compartment to open now, it would be lees work for you, other think, the doors are not open by those nuts of all-around, this are only to put the tap for the doors. To open the doors is a little easier, do you see that hole there in for of a cross there? You will need to build a tool with that form, but that the form of cross start from down there to inside, you have to measure the deep and make the tool the same size, no more or less of that deep.

Now the thinks are more at sight, the fist is to build that part, so he went to his truck and bring a measuring tape, measure the long the wide and the deep in the cross, also measure the gross of the metal wall to find out de deep that the cross of the tool need to have, and with that information, go to the industrial shop that manufacture the necessary parts in order to repair the machineries for the industries in the island. And ask to manufacture that tool, the details of how it should be, and say that only need to make only one, because that tool is not in use too much, but that rarely will be in use, only some times, and maybe no more.

In the shop he was said to relax, they notice him something tense. Take like two days vacation, because that is not an ease to make tool, it should be build of titanium, because maybe need to make some force to make move whatever the mechanism be, maybe is oxide with the time, and titanium melt at 5,000 grades Celsius and must to make it in foundation, because titanium is very difficult to sold, and where you sold it, brakes easily, if it brake would need to make another one, is unfixed.

Come in two days to pick it up, today is Friday, on Monday very early will be ready and cold, will be able to take anyplace, with your own hands if pick it up on Monday night, will be still hot and will need to pick it up with something else, we need to be careful with the hot metals, cannot add water to cool it off, because will lose part of its hardiness, and when apply force the metal could not stay rect, but It will twist. The tool will not get damage because of that, but it be good for anything because the tool must to hold when you apply force to be able to move the mechanism, is like to try to move the mechanism with a tool made out of vegetal cords.

Monday morning after breakfast, Worm address himself to the industrial shop, and his tool is ready, can hold it directly with his hand to put it in the truck and star to work, opening the doors and find the generator of electricity of that he doesn't know anything, so he expect to find a diagram of the construction of it, from what he does know, how to read. His father in remote time was a school teacher teacher of.

At time to get to the hill, her mother accompany him until the ship, and he told her to stay and make him company, your company will give me the peace I need to do what I need to do.

Rupert – I can do that, give you peace and put you some conversation for you find that peace you need now. My company is the best that you can have, you would not have anything better, that accompany you and to be at your side all the time you want me in your company.

Start to open doors, really it was not an extraordinary power, just a little push on the beginning, the rest move softly, he open 20 doors, what took until noon, then his mother said, the lunch is ready and served, and need to come to enjoy, stop that work, once he know he had found the generator or power fount of the machine, but to work with it and the ship can cost him a lot of time before put it to work, before go, took a view around and found a diagram of the circuits, and were very quiet because at least now where to start to search for the damage, to be able to fix it.

For lunch he light very much to find his brother Robert, who was looking for him, and was looking for him and calling to his cellular and he did not answered.

Robert – Nobody answer me, so I know when you get lose was here were you are, I came to get you, I have one hour that came, but nobody now where you were or what direction have take, because nobody was looking when you left. So simply do not know.

It was a lot of happiness there, and forgot completely they were fixing the space ship, and got concentrated in the conversation with Roberto and his friend, who has come to ask to Worm. Also forgot that they need to go back to finish to put the ship in operation, beside of return the electricity to the streets, That had been disconnect the electricity of the zone that les obstruct the normal life of the isle, because it was the zone that was the zone that only affect to the family of Worm.

Robert friend consult to Worm his matter and this answer to him living it resolved, then they went back to el Pedregal, Worm took a delicious coffee with spice and came back to find the explanation he desire to know, and that already was not that not that nasty because that will know as soon as make electricity into the ship, the only door needed to be opened by electricity was the direct access to the interiors of the ship, all those the others give access to the service area or cargo, that was connected with the ship by doors also electric, soon was open the door with access to the generator, a generator small, small like 2 feet high, 1 foot in the front, and 4 feet long, that was the size of the generator, that produced the half of the electricity of the all island that use to consume 16 millions of kHz that was working in parallel with 16 generators hydroelectric and together supply the all island which demand was like 16 millions or kava. All that power in such a little space, and better greater. The electric connection is done in base to the theories of a mister call Nikola Tessla who say that the all atmosphere was load with positive energy and the land was charged with negative energy. All those theories finishing in that is was possible make all that electricity without to expend o even a drop of fuel of expense. Because that was electricity which coming from the air where come from the sun, cloudy or sunny. The sun is always charging the atmosphere, of the earth, for over the clouds, and this us communicated with the atmosphere below, and when is night the sun light the other face of the earth, so, is communicated all the time, for which do never get discharged.

Our Worm was in front to the wonder of the generator of electricity and note that a system of interruption of the electricity of the machine is off, will be that someone discovered that machine, turn it off, and put all again as it was? Because no cable come out of the ship there is no connection at all at least not as cable we know, at least to be invisible or unwired like ray x, how may this work? Says Worm to himself, besides he say it will be better to study the plan of the ship, in particular of the machine, to understand get to see the diagram first of how produce electricity, and then how it is connected with the exterior, in order to get an idea of how it Is connect, and disconnected, the machine to the exterior.

In that order note in the electric diagram there is a circuit that can connected or disconnected manually, but also a receptacle to use with remote control and connect this machine, but is very strong and is capable to trespass the titanium wall of the ship. As to himself who may have access to that kind of remote control? And put to play with it, turn off the generator the machine, because who turn off. First have to know about it and then to know how to use it. I need to talk this with my mother; the key should be around these. Meanwhile, connect manually the circuits to turn on the ship and return the production of electricity that keep on the streets and highways of the country at night time.

At arrive the night, Worm can see all the island how lighted it is lighted, inclusive his way to return home, but do not want yet, open the door and enter the ship, turn on the screen and once ear talking, is seen the figure of a man of white color with 40 years of age, and the voice say:

"Hello, I cannot imagine that it be another person present here, beyond minw loved elder son Worm, because I arranged everything for when accomplished the majority of age and had the adult tries, and have the maturity enough to understand all the world that surround you, and can understand the nature of the world that surround you. During many years have live in a wonderful world, but that you do not understand, because you are not equal to the others, you are the son that is not either same as the others, I am a man, I am not a God, not either a son of God, as consequently either you are so.

You are a special man, as your father, is an special man, I am a prophet of God and as such, enjoy of the power of God, for to do good to wherever I go, nobody can destroy me while I act as God want wishes, because in my surroundings there are tools put to defend us, as you too have them, on the other side, enjoy of have the two women wonderful, plenty of health and full of the love for God, and I have left to both plenty with my love also, because I love to both, I love to both, and I love them still, from my home beyond the clouds. That ship have some system automatics, have the route saved in the navigation system to bring you to me in case you want to come some day to share something besides if you want to stay there, I understand, and accept, but to you and your brother only can imagine, because I could fix and build my machine in fast time, very fast, and did not see bird to Roberto, but only you, only can imagine how you will look now.

You know more of me than me of you, I can know how you are, because I know the can of education that could accept and know that your mother do not educate you from a different way, because she love me and will show respect to me always .that is how you are, you are my first born, and for to inherit my powers and mine work for to the sky, it is necessary to be first born, but your brother have your qualities, if you come to me, no matter its be temporarily your brother can substitute you in your labor while you are absent, in that way was the program prepared.

But I left it to your election, I did not intervened at all, no matter I want more than all, in the world to hug you and give you my love I gave to your mother, and your aunt who I loved and I love still, whom I met virgin, and they were only for me, those that were only for me, those which also gave all their love during those 2 years that I live for them. Until here will this conversation last, because that is how I want you have take it also, and that only you have listened, I from here lived listen to you, every time I talk to some one of your age, or your brothers when I see go every time, until ever my dear and loved elder son, I love you.

Worm star the motor of the ship and this sound like a hiss. Like two metal flat plates, that turn in their race one to the other, race it and it goes rounding around but only in the exterior with all the herb that can pick up from the earth softly go to the end of the gravity force have its effect that is like 10 kilometers and go and park in the football stadium of football in the capitol. Over there go a great deal of people, they stop to contemplate that wonderful apparatus, and that before that wonderful machine, before show up, the all electric system was restored, The 200 marines that were restored in all the island, appeared his commander and call to the pentagon, and informed of the existence of that machine flat that fly as is described those flats plates which travel to phantasmal speed, and that have too great powers.

Worm makes that exhibition of his fling machine, only to the island know it, but at any moment was considering that the country was full of oats, and that will be reported in the foreign and to whom they treat from the best way, to whom have offered and deliver a life of the best category in exchange for nothing only for the placer of seem them happy, and now they are betraying as really patriots, and Worm knew that in the moment that something like that happening it has to repatriate them they had a list of the foreign that had nationalized,

Worm return to the house of his mother, now park the spaceship where it can be see, dismount and go to the house and ask about the remote control, she say that she has it and it was she who turned the motor off the electric generator because she had realize you already had the age of to understand everything, and that you get to know your father. He had instructed in do it that way, that when he was, the ship produced the electricity for the all island, because they do not produced devise for the all thing and to buy fuel, because the generators, at the beginning were working, but little by little were stop using, in the way that were building, hydroelectric and that these produced the necessary electricity in case of the ship is gone or damaged.

The first that occur to Worm is to prepare the island for to resist without it, so that the computer now with the remote control that is the remote control that is the cellular phone interspatial, and that can communicate with his father in the planet where he lived, his mother did use that apparatus to talk to the father of Worm and that her sister also talk to him sometimes, as for example once a year.

Worm calls his father and have a long conversation with him

Worm – I do not see this cellular phone connected to any thing, and I do not see it has any batteries of any kind.

Rupert – That equipment is connected to the electric system permanently, but wireless, you are the negative cable and the positive is connected with an antenna that the radio has internal. Mr. Tessla discover those technology, and he knew them on earth during the time I lived there, those invent were never registered, and beside that, he never had families, not wife, not a heir, nothing, for that nobody may prohibit its use or put limitations over those.

Well, now the things are putting complicated, Because at been turn on the ship, and put to fly, give as consequence that the dome of protection disappear, to put again the dome, need to turn off the generator, because the dome putted and the generator connected, need to turn the generator off, because they together, they only work together until you give a restart to the generator, for that my mother turn it off and do not turned on again, if not that let Worm to turn it on, because this could connect inside of the ship.

The gringos realized of there was not dome, and prepare a great invasion, with about 10,000 planes American, French, German, English, Japanese, Italian, an invasion enormous, and dispatch the invasion immediately, now with the objective of take the ship, that ship build by extraterrestrial, and whit technology of latest technology would be an extraordinary interest.

The sky of the island turn silver color with all those planes in the air, beside of make a too grate shade, because to fit in the island, they need to fly one on top of the other, because they occupy more space of the space of the complete island, they of course cannot land all at the same time, because they do not fit, not even like harriers or like helicopter, so, they plan to use this system, for the last time.

The president of the isle do not know where to address, then, was waiting that the chief of state and the expedition call to impose conditions in the palace of govern. Those do not make themselves to hope, and in one hour arrive and nock the door of the door of palace in the isle, which would open only if the joint will come together in other to retain more efficiently the air conditioned.

Chief of invaders – Mr. President, we will not go by the top, we have to take with us to our country the space ship that land here yesterday and that you have no right to retained.

President of the island – That ship had been there for more than 20 years, and is his proprietor who used yesterday, you know him perfectly to the man proprietor of it, who receipt it in this day as his inheritance from his own father and only came out for a raid of taste, he would like, he could destroy to all of you together, but he did not want to, because he is a man of peace, I remind you, that now is too excited to do such a thing.

Will continue

www.ingramcontent.com/pod-product-compliance
Lightning Source LLC
Chambersburg PA
CBHW071419180526
45170CB00001B/149